CHRIST IN OUR PLACE

Genehmigt von der theologischen Fakultät auf Antrag
der Herren Prof. Karl Barth, Referent, Prof. Hendrick
van Oyen, Coreferent.

Basel, den 30. Jan., 1954   Der Dekan Herr Prof.
                                 OSCAR CULLMANN

A doctoral dissertation submitted to the Theological
Faculty of the University of Basel.

CHRIST IN OUR PLACE

The Substitutionary Character of
Calvin's Doctrine of Reconciliation

BY

PAUL van BUREN

Wm. B. Eerdmans Publishing Company
Grand Rapids, Michigan

FIRST PUBLISHED . . . 1957

Published in Britain by Oliver & Boyd

PHOTOLITHOPRINTED BY CUSHING - MALLOY, INC.
ANN ARBOR, MICHIGAN, UNITED STATES OF AMERICA

FOREWORD

THE foundation of the Christian faith is the person and work of Jesus Christ. Yet Christians today are often unable 'to give answer to every man that asks (them) a reason concerning the hope that is in (them)' (1 Pet. 3.15), precisely because they are uncertain about this foundation. It is typical of Christians today to feel that such matters as the doctrine of the person of Christ were settled at Church Councils long ago and need not be reopened, and that the question of just *how* Christ has reconciled us to God is one of those mysteries about which nothing solid may be established and which must simply be left as a conviction of faith that 'somehow' we are saved by the Cross of Christ. The modern Christian feels that it is his responsibility to concern himself with more timely and pressing problems, such as the doctrines of the ministry, the Sacraments and the Church, or with the questions of the social action and witness of the Church in the areas of politics and human relations in general. It is not to be denied that these are important concerns for every Christian, but we cannot concern ourselves with these matters without first of all working out towards them from the centre of reality and of our faith, the person and work of Jesus Christ. In fact, it is a question whether there exists any difference of opinion or conviction between Christians and Churches on such matters that does not actually have its roots in a difference in their understanding of the person and work of Christ. This study in Calvin has strengthened my conviction that as Christ is the centre of our faith, so Christology is the *determining* centre of all theology. If we are not sound at this point, if we do not consciously make it *our* foundation, but set it aside as having been settled by the Church before us, then our building will be in vain.

Few Christians have had a greater influence than Calvin upon the thinking and theology of the Church. Not only was he the acknowledged theological leader in that side of the Reformation

vii

which was later to be called 'Reformed', in distinction to the Lutherans, but his influence was also felt in my own communion, the Anglican. Whether one chooses to agree with Calvin or not, one is obliged to take seriously a theologian of such wide influence. And yet there are few men in the history of the Church who are so misunderstood today. The scholastic orthodoxy of the seventeenth century Reformed theologians has left us a heritage of 'Calvinism' in which it is only with difficulty that one can recognize Calvin himself. Yet the theology that guided the Reformation in Geneva, France and the Netherlands, and had many direct and indirect influences in Scotland and also in England, was not 'Calvinism' but the theology of Calvin. Those of us who are members of those parts of the one Catholic, Church which were to a greater or lesser degree reformed and purified in the sixteenth century would do well to know more about this reformation, not simply for its historical interest, but because we believe in one Church, in time as well as geographically, and are therefore called to listen with respect to those who have gone before us in the faith as well as to our contemporaries. Because we believe in one Church, we must remain in conversation with the Church Fathers, the mediaeval scholastics, and also with the Reformers, as well as with our contemporaries.

Ultimately, it was a personal choice that led me to select Calvin for this study, based partly on an admiration for the order and clarity of his work but also partly on a sense of dissatisfaction with Calvin and a desire to know what it was about his thought that struck a discordant note, why it was that so much of what he said struck home with such effectiveness, whereas other parts left me dissatisfied. I had only a knowledge of the *Institutes* when I started the investigation, and I was later to discover through the study of his *Commentaries* on the Old and New Testaments that much that had seemed difficult and unacceptable before became clear and convincing once one had seen the breadth of the man's thought, a breadth that is not always immediately apparent if one confines oneself to the orderly *Institutes*. Surprisingly enough Calvin has not been widely studied in our time. Luther, for example, has been carefully studied in this century, yet there are many and important elements in Calvin's theology that remain untouched and largely forgotten. This lack of attention to Calvin must account for the fact that so few people realize to what an extent we are indebted to the man. For example, it has been interesting to me as an Episcopalian to discover that our liturgy of Holy Communion is a very good presentation of what Calvin taught about the Lord's Supper. Yet how often is this noticed today?

Calvin's understanding of our reconciliation to God in the person and work of Christ would, however, have been too vast a subject to handle with the degree of scholarship demanded of a doctoral dissertation, and I was forced to narrow the field. I did this by concentrating on the theological centre of the doctrine of Reconciliation: the work of Christ, which became the main section of the study, Part II. But what began as a study of the work of Christ became more and more an investigation of the substitutionary or representative character of Christ in that work, simply because that is the fundamental element of Christ's work in Calvin's reading of Scripture. In this central section, as elsewhere, my concern was to understand and present Calvin himself, letting him speak in his own words as much as possible, but in order to clarify what Calvin was saying I compared his teaching with that of the men who shaped the theology of the Church of Calvin's time and which he worked to reform: Peter Lombard's *Sententiae*, the mediaeval textbook of theology, and the *Summa* of Aquinas, the crown of the scholastic development of that theology. I added Anselm to the list because of the importance of his work for the theology of the Atonement. I might, of course, have gone further afield, adding Augustine and Bernard of Clairvaux, both of whom Calvin quotes with approval in other contexts, but the purpose of this comparison was not to offer a comparative study of Calvin and the theology of the Church preceding him but to present what Calvin himself had to say. For the same reason I have not entered into a comparative study of Calvin with the other Reformers or with his Roman or sectarian opponents. The purpose of choosing a few of the theologians of the age preceding the Reformation was simply to help to clarify Calvin's own teaching, which of course has its place within the continuing tradition of the Church's theological work, for I felt that it was my task to present Calvin himself rather than make a study of his place within the history and development of Christian doctrine. These comparisons are, moreover, confined to the footnotes, in order to leave the text free for the presentation of Calvin himself.

Having concentrated on the very heart of the doctrine of Reconciliation, the Atonement, I had to show how Calvin arrived at this centre. (I use the word 'reconciliation' here and throughout this study in the broad sense that it has come to have today, indicating the whole area of the reconciliation of men to God by way of the Incarnation, the life and the death of Christ, and its realization through the work of the Spirit. Calvin used it in a narrower sense, referring simply to justification.) Part I, therefore, had to present summarily the problem of sinful man confronted by the righteousness of God, and God's solution of this problem in the Incarnation of His Son, upon which the Atonement rests. Finally, in Part III, it was necessary to present the subjective side of reconciliation as it follows from its objective foundation in the person and work of Christ, in order to remain true to Calvin. Here my intention was only to sketch the general way in which Calvin follows out from this centre. Thus, for example, I could not give a full presentation of such matters as sanctification, justification, the Church and the Sacraments, but could only show how these questions were understood by Calvin to be based on the central doctrine of the person and work of Christ. If one wanted to understand Calvin's doctrine of the Church, it would be insufficient to read Book IV of the *Institutes* without Book II. It is this connection that I have tried to make clear.

These, then, are the reasons for the order and construction of this study in Calvin. As for the method, Calvin himself has determined that for me. Having presented a *summa* of his theology in the final edition of the *Institutes*, he requires us to follow that as our primary source, letting it determine both the content and the order of presentation. But I have also made extensive use of his *Commentaries* to indicate the fullness of his thought at every step of the way. I did not use the sermons because I found again and again that these contained other ways of saying what I had already found in the *Commentaries* and provided no essentially new material. In the footnotes I have indicated my sources by chapter and verse for the *Institutes* and for the *Commentaries*, for those who have translations but for whom the *Corpus Reformatorum* might not be so readily available. I have of course made my own translations for the sake of precise faithfulness to the original texts, and so the wording of published translations may not be exactly the same as that of my quotations.

Finally, the reader will find a criticism of Calvin's theology running through the whole of this study. The basis of this criticism is, however, neither a confessional norm nor a supposedly biblical theology but Calvin himself. That is to say, the criticism that I have felt it necessary to make consists of a series of questions that have presented themselves out of Calvin's own theology. I did not feel that it was my place, in presenting Calvin's thought, to reject him at any point or to offer what I happened to regard as better alternatives, but I did feel that I owed it to a responsible presentation to point up the questions of Calvin's theology in such a way that the reader had before him in the form of Calvin's own words the material with which to examine the problems that exist within Calvin's thought. In this way I have sought to be fair to Calvin and to use him as he would have us use him in a Church that has accepted as its norm and canon, not Calvin or any other theologian, but only the biblical witness to Jesus Christ.

Before turning to our subject I want to take this opportunity of expressing my deepest and warmest thanks to Professor Karl Barth for his interest, encouragement and most helpful suggestions during the preparation of this study.

PAUL VAN BUREN

Basel, *27th February* 1954

CONTENTS

PART III

INCORPORATION: UNION WITH CHRIST

PART I

THE INCARNATION: CHRIST'S UNION WITH US

CHAPTER I

THE CAUSE OF THE INCARNATION

1. THE NEED FOR A MEDIATOR

CALVIN'S doctrine of Reconciliation is an expansion of his compact statement that, in order to be reconciled to God, it was necessary that man, 'who had ruined himself by his disobedience, should remedy his condition by obedience, should satisfy the justice of God, and suffer the punishment for his sin. Our Lord, then, made His appearance as a real man; He put on the character of Adam and assumed his name, to act as his substitute in his obedience to the Father, to lay down our flesh as the price of satisfaction to the justice of God, and to suffer in the same flesh the punishment which we had deserved.'[1] The fulcrum of this passage is substitution: Christ in our place. But in order to make clear the substitutionary character of Christ's work it is necessary to review Calvin's doctrine of the Incarnation, that it may be evident who is our Substitute, how and why He took our place, and the extent to which He took our place.

Calvin begins his treatment of the doctrine of Reconciliation with the problem of fallen man.[2] It is not self-evident, however, that this should have been his starting place. Calvin has established in Book I of his *Institutes* that the knowledge of God must precede the knowledge of man,[3] and that it is precisely this knowledge of God that has been lost to man,[4] and which now can be recovered only by means of God's Word, faithfully heard.[5] *In* Christ, that is, we learn what we were *out of* Christ. Would it not have been better, therefore, to begin with the solution rather

---

[1] *Instit.* II.12.3, C.R. 30, 341-342.

[2] *Instit.* II, the first five chapters.

[3] 'Hominem in purem sui notitiam nunquam pervenire constat nisi prius Dei faciem sit contemplatus.' *Instit.* I.1.2, C.R. 30, 32.

[4] 'Porro sive alii evanescant in suis superstitionibus, sive alii data opera malitiose a Deo desciscant, omnes tamen degerant a vera eius notitia.' *Instit.* I.4.1, C.R. 30, 38.

[5] *Instit.* I.6.2, C.R. 30, 53 seq.

3

than with the problem? Would it not have been more consistent with what he says if Calvin had presented the *event* of reconciliation first, and then shown the necessity for reconciliation, a necessity that is only to be understood in the light of the event itself? It is true that there are many passages in which he does just that: 'If we were firmly persuaded of what, indeed, ought not to be questioned, that our nature is destitute of all those things which our heavenly Father confers on His elect through the Spirit of regeneration, there would be no cause for hesitation here.'[1] And again: 'If the death of Christ be our redemption, then we were captives; if it be satisfaction, we were debtors; if it be atonement, we were guilty; if it be cleansing, we were unclean.'[2] Yet in his definitive edition of his *Institutes* Calvin chose to present the doctrine of sin first, with Christology following as the solution to this problem. It may be that he saw the problem of man's fallen condition as a solved problem, speaking of man-apart-from-Christ from the point of view of man-in-Christ. If that is true, then it is unfortunate that he did not make this clearer in the structure of the *Institutes*, a misfortune to which the history of Protestant theology bears witness.

The starting point, then, is human sin, which Calvin sees essentially as disobedience.[3] Tempted by Satan, man disobeyed God's command, thereby introducing disorder into God's creation.[4] This primal act of disobedience was Adam's, but we were also involved in it, for Adam, as the first man, bore a representational character. He was created as the father of the whole human race, and in dealing with him God was at the same time dealing with us all. Thus, what Adam received from God he received for us all: 'The Lord deposited with Adam the gifts He chose to confer on human nature. Therefore, when he lost that which he had received, he lost them not only for himself, but also for us.'[5] Adam's sin is also ours, not by a biological transmission but because in Adam God was dealing with all men: 'for the corruption of all mankind in the person of Adam alone did not

[1] *Instit.* II.2.20, *C.R.* 30, 201.
[2] *Comm. in Gal.* 2.21, *C.R.* 78, 200-201. Cf. *in Eph.* 1.10, *C.R.* 79, 151; *in Isa.* 42.1, *C.R.* 65, 59-60; *in Act.* 10.43, *C.R.* 76, 249; *in* 1 *Joh.* 4.10, *C.R.* 83, 354.
[3] *Instit.* II.1.4, *C.R.* 30, 178.
[4] Ibid. Cf. *Comm. in Gen.* 3.1, *C.R.* 51, 55.
[5] *Instit.* II.1.7, *C.R.* 30, 181.

proceed from generation, but from the appointment of God, who in one man had adorned us all, and who has in him also deprived us of his gifts'.[1] Following Romans 5.12, Calvin points out that we are not innocent creatures who have been loaded with the guilt of another; we have all followed our representative in the path of disobedience. 'We derive from him not only the punishment but also a pollution within us which justly deserves the punishment',[2] and thus all men are made 'liable to punishment by their own sinfulness, not by the sinfulness of another'.[3]

All men stand as sinners before God, under the curse and the punishment of death. The problem, therefore, arises from this condition of mankind, in which through our own fault we are all in revolt against, and separated from, Him who is Life. 'Since our iniquities, intervening between us and Him like a cloud, had alienated us from the Kingdom of Heaven, no one could be a mediator for the restoration of peace except Him who could approach God', an office which could not be undertaken by any of the children of Adam, for 'they, with their parent, all dreaded the divine presence'.[4] The distance that lies between the holy God and sinful men is far too great for us to find the way across, for not only is there the difference between the Creator and His creatures, but now there is added the barrier of sin. 'Although man had remained immaculately innocent, yet his condition would have been too mean for him to approach God without a mediator. What then can he do after having been plunged by his fatal fall into death and Hell, defiled with so many blemishes, putrefied in his own corruption, and in a word overwhelmed with every curse?'[5] Calvin takes man's disobedience and revolt seriously. It is a condition of his being 'wholly at variance with God', of being 'His enemy'.[6] 'Since the word *enemies* has a passive as well as an active meaning, it is well suited to us in both respects, so long as we are apart from Christ. For we are both children of wrath from birth, and every thought of the flesh is against God.'[7] And this condition extends to every man, so that all are in need of reconciliation to God.[8] If we find this judgment too hard, then we are only seeing things by the world's standards rather than

---

[1] *Comm. in Joh.* 3.6, *C.R.* 75, 57.
[2] *Instit.* II.1.8, *C.R.* 30, 182.
[3] *Instit.* II.1.8, *C.R.* 30, 183.
[4] *Instit.* II.12.1, *C.R.* 30, 340.
[5] Ibid.
[6] *Comm. in Col.* 1.21, *C.R.* 80, 90.
[7] Ibid.
[8] *Comm. in Joh.* 1.29, *C.R.* 75, 26.

according to the truth of God. 'But the apostle assumes this as a sure axiom of Scripture (of which these profane sophists are ignorant), that we are born so corrupt and depraved that there is in us as it were an innate hatred of God, so that we desire nothing but what is displeasing to Him, all the passions of our flesh carrying on continual war with His righteousness.'[1]

From the side of man, then, the situation is hopeless. All that we had possessed, we had possessed by our 'participation in God'.[2] This has now been lost, as well as all hope of returning to the source of our life.[3] And that not by anyone's fault but our own, for we have put ourselves in revolt against the source of all our blessings. We have set up our sin as a barrier to keep ourselves away from God. 'The whole may be summed up thus: where sin is, there is the wrath of God, and therefore God is not propitious to us without, or before, His blotting out our sins.'[4] In need of restoration to God, we have no way of reaching Him, or, in fact, even of wanting restoration.[5] There could be only one source of help in this situation: God Himself would have to come to the aid of His revolting creatures. 'Our situation was truly deplorable unless the divine Majesty itself would descend to us, for we could not ascend to it. Thus it was necessary that the Son of God should become Immanuel, that is, God with us.'[6]

2. THE GIFT OF A MEDIATOR

As seriously as Calvin takes the Fall of man, he never for a moment regards it as a fall out of the realm of God's love. Although fallen, man remains God's creature and the object of His love. 'He loved us gratuitously, even before we were born, and also when, through depravity of nature, we had hearts turned against Him, yielding to no right or godly feelings.'[7] Had God

---

[1] *Comm. in* 1 *Joh.* 4.10, *C.R.* 83, 353.

[2] *Instit.* II.2.1, *C.R.* 30, 186. 'In the first place, let us consider that our happiness consists in our cleaving to God, and on the other hand there is nothing more miserable than to be alienated from Him.' *Comm. in Col.* 1.20, *C.R.* 80, 88.

[3] 'Christ shows that we are all dead before He quickens us, and hence it is clear what the whole nature of man can accomplish towards procuring salvation.' *Comm. in Joh.* 5.25, *C.R.* 75, 117.

[4] *Comm. in* 2 *Cor.* 5.19, *C.R.* 78, 72.

[5] 'We shun and dread every access to Him unless a mediator comes who can deliver us from fear.' *Comm. in* 1 *Pet.* 1.21, *C.R.* 83, 226.

[6] *Instit.* II.12.1, *C.R.* 30, 340.   [7] *Comm. in* 1 *Joh.* 4.10, *C.R.* 83, 353.

not loved fallen man, no possibility would have remained for salvation. Therefore, Calvin insists, 'our reconciliation by the death of Christ must not be understood as if the Son reconciled us to (the Father) that He might begin to love those whom He had before hated; but we were reconciled to Him who already loved us, but with whom we were at enmity on account of sin'.[1] Reconciliation through Christ is based on God's eternal love, which precedes in time and in order the event of reconciliation: 'God did not begin to love us when we were reconciled to Him by the blood of His Son, but He loved us before the creation of the world.'[2]

We are the object of reconciliation, not God. He is the activator of the reconciliation of sinful men to Himself, the motivation for this activity on His part being nothing other than the nature of God Himself, for 'He will never find in us anything which He ought to love, but He loves us because He is good and merciful'.[3] Thus the very first thing to be said about our salvation is that it is all the work of God's eternal love for His sinful creatures: 'The love of God precedes our reconciliation in Christ; indeed, because He first loves (1 John 4.19), He afterwards reconciles us to Himself.'[4] But this prior and eternal love of God's does not eliminate His wrath against sin, and against man in so far as he is a sinner. Calvin quotes Augustine with approval: God 'both hated and loved us at the same time. He hated us being different from what He had made us; but as our iniquity had not destroyed entirely His work in us, He could at the same time in every one of us hate what we had done and love what He had made.'[5] In his own words, Calvin puts it this way: 'God does not detest in us His own workmanship—that is, that He has made us men—but our uncleanness, which has extinguished the light of His image.'[6] In terms of this barrier of sin, therefore, there is a sense in which Calvin is able to speak of God as the object of reconciliation: by the event of our reconciliation to Him, God is able to remove the barrier that stood in the way of the full exercise of His love for us, a barrier that we had erected and

---

[1] *Instit.* II.16.4, *C.R.* 30, 370.   [2] Ibid.
[3] *Comm. in Tit.* 3.4, *C.R.* 80, 429. ' . . . *a seipso causam petens cur illi bene-faciat, quod peccatorum ipsum bonitatis suae sensu afficiat.*' *Instit.* III.11.16, *C.R.* 30, 547.
[4] *Instit.* II.16.3, *C.R.* 30, 370.   [5] *Instit.* II.16.4, *C.R.* 30, 370.
[6] *Comm. in Rom.* 3.25, *C.R.* 77, 62.

which only He could remove. 'To remove every obstacle in the
way of His love for us, God appointed a method of salvation in
Christ. . . . For God in a certain inexpressible manner àt the same
time that He loved us was nevertheless angry with us, until He
was reconciled in Christ.'[1]   This means, then, that for Calvin the
gift of reconciliation reveals the true nature of God.   In Christ
God establishes Himself and reveals to men what He is in all
eternity: 'It is a common way of speaking in the Scriptures that
the world was reconciled to God by the death of Christ, although
we know that He was a kind Father in all ages.   But because we
find no cause for the love of God towards us and no ground for
our salvation but in Christ, it is not without good reason that
God the Father is said to have shown His goodness to us in Him.'[2]
The Father is Himself the Reconciler, therefore, for it was He
who 'appointed this method of salvation for us'.[3]

The gift of the Mediator is the realization of God's eternal
love[4] and therefore the final revelation of God's eternal will:
'It was from God's goodness alone as from a fountain that
Christ with all his blessings has come to us. . . . Hence all who
inquire apart from Christ what is determined for them in God's
secret counsel are mad to their own ruin.'[5]   It is not our intention to analyse Calvin's doctrine of predestination, that which
'is determined for them in God's secret counsel' (which in the
Institutes, be it noted, follows *after* all that he has to say about
Christ, His work, and the Christian life, and is therefore presented as a clarification of what has gone before), but a question
may be raised here.   Did Calvin really mean that election is to be
understood in terms of Christ alone?   And if God's decision about
every man has been made in Christ, as Calvin seems to say here,
why does he speak of a counsel of God that is 'secret' and as it
were hidden behind or above Christ?

Calvin stresses the priority of God's love by calling it the
originating or primary cause (*summa causa*) of our salvation.[6]

[1] *Instit.* II.17.2, *C.R.* 30, 387.   [2] *Comm. in Tit.* 3.4, *C.R.* 80, 428.
[3] *Instit.* II.17.1, *C.R.* 30, 387.   'God of Himself willingly sought out a means
by which He might take away our curse.'   *Comm. in Rom.* 3.25, *C.R.* 77, 62.
[4] 'Christ has now appeared for our salvation, not because this power has been
given to Him recently, but because this grace was laid up in Him for us before
the creation of the world.'   *Comm. in 2 Tim.* 1.10, *C.R.* 80, 353.
[5] *Comm. in 1 Joh.* 4.10, *C.R.* 83, 353-354.
[6] *Instit.* II.17.2, *C.R.* 30, 387.   Cf. III.14.17, *C.R.* 30, 575; III.14.21, *C.R.*
30, 578.

That is, God's reconciling love is grounded in Himself, in the inner life of the triune God. The form of this reconciling love is the love of the Father for the Son, and it is by this love that we are to measure the love of God for us. 'Surely this is a notable and rich proof of inestimable love, that the Father has not refused to bestow His Son upon our salvation.'[1] Here we only touch on what will concern us in detail later, that God's love for men is none other than the Father's love for the Son. 'For if the death of Christ is the pledge of God's love towards us, it follows that *even then we were acceptable* to Him; but now (Paul) says we were enemies. I answer, because God hates sin we are also odious to Him in so far as we are sinners; but as in His secret counsel He elects us *into the body of Christ*, He ceases to hate us.'[2] God loves us in Christ with the love that He has for the Son.

In the gift of the Mediator, therefore, we have the revelation of God Himself, giving Himself to men as their redeemer.[3] In Christ 'the love of God is poured out upon us',[4] for God is the giver of this gift. He is not 'a mere spectator, but the author of our salvation'.[5] That is, the gift of a mediator is the revelation of God's love in the fullest sense of the word, for the Mediator is none other than God Himself, giving Himself to us in His way of being as the eternal Son: 'The most merciful God, when he determined upon our redemption, became himself our Redeemer in the *persona* of the only-begotten Son.'[6] Therefore, in the Mediator we have to do with God Himself. 'It is evident that we cannot believe in God except through Christ, in whom God in a manner makes Himself small, that he may accommodate Himself to our comprehension.'[7] And the God with whom we have to do here is a God who is *pro nobis*. 'We ought not to look at anything else in Christ, therefore, than the fact that God out of His boundless goodness chose to extend His help to save us who were lost.'[8] There can be no thought, therefore, of any opposition between the Father and the Son in Calvin's understanding of the Atonement. The unity of the Father and the Son is a reciprocal love that finds expression in the perfect obedience of the Son to the Father, and an obedience that is free and

[1] *Comm. in Rom.* 8.32, C.R. 77, 163.　　[2] *Comm. in Rom.* 5.10, C.R. 77, 94.
[3] '*Dominus . . . in Christi facie redemptor apparet.*' *Instit.* I.2.1, C.R. 30, 34.
[4] *Comm. in Eph.* 1.5, C.R. 79, 149. Cf. *in Eph.* 1.7, C.R. 79, 150.
[5] *Instit.* III.22.6, C.R. 30, 692.　　[6] *Instit.* II.12.2, C.R. 30, 341.
[7] *Comm. in 1 Pet.* 1.21, C.R. 83, 227.　　[8] *Comm. in Joh.* 3.17, C.R. 75, 66.

voluntary.[1] God as Father and as Son has reconciled the world to Himself, and the saving work ascribed to Christ in the Bible is, Calvin insists, 'with equal propriety ascribed in other parts of Scripture to God the Father, for on the one hand the Father decreed this atonement by an eternal purpose and gave this proof of His love to us, that he did not spare his only-begotten Son, but delivered Him up for us; and Christ on the other hand offered Himself as a sacrifice in order to reconcile us to God'.[2] Reconciliation came by the work of the Son, but it depended first of all on the Father's gift of a mediator. 'As the whole matter of our salvation must not be sought anywhere else but in Christ, so we must see whence Christ came to us and why He was offered to be our Saviour. Both points are distinctly stated to us: namely, that faith in Christ brings life to all, and that Christ brought life because the Heavenly Father loves the human race and wishes that it should not perish.'[3]

---

[1] *Comm. in Joh.* 14.31, *C.R.* 75, 338. Cf. *in Phil.* 2.8. *C.R.* 80, 27. This will be considered in detail in Part II.

[2] *Comm. in Gal.* 1.4, *C.R.* 78, 170.

[3] *Comm. in Joh.* 3.16, *C.R.* 75, 63-64.

CHAPTER II

THE INCARNATE

1. THE DIVINITY OF CHRIST

THE Mediator given to us by the Father is God the eternal
Son, of one essence with the Father,[1] who is 'Himself the
eternal and essential Word of the Father',[2] the same Word
who was always the Mediator and through whom God dealt with,
and appeared to, the Patriarchs before the Incarnation.[3] The
Son, therefore, is God in His self-revelation: 'As all divinely given
revelations are rightly called "the Word of God", so we ought
chiefly to reckon as the source of all revelations Him who is
substantially the Word, who is liable to no variation, who remains
with God perpetually one and the same, and who is God Himself.'[4] The Mediator comes to us from the side of God, not from
our side, so that in Him we confront the One to whom we need
to be reconciled, in all His divine majesty; 'for who of us does not
dread the sight of the Son of God, especially when we consider
what our condition is and when our sins come to mind?'[5]

But the Son is the incarnate Mediator, not the Father. For
men, the Son is one God with the Father, but within the Godhead He is distinct,[6] so that although the Son is 'the Lord of life
and death, nevertheless He became obedient to His Father, even
so far as to endure death'.[7] But this work of obedience to which
He was sent 'was destined by the eternal decree of God',[8] so that
in this distinction of *personae* we must not try to find any separation or opposition. The Incarnation of the Son is the expression
of the eternal will of God: 'Christ's becoming our Redeemer and
His participation in the same nature (with us) have been connected

---

[1] 'For where can there be equality with God without robbery excepting
only where there is the essence of God?' *Comm. in Phil.* 2.6, C.R. 80, 25.
[2] *Instit.* I.13.7, C.R. 30, 95.
[3] *Instit.* I.13.10, C.R. 30, 98.   [4] *Instit.* I.13.7, C.R. 30, 95.
[5] *Comm. in Heb.* 4.15, C.R. 83, 53.   [6] *Instit.* I.13.19, C.R. 30, 105-106.
[7] *Comm. in Phil.* 2.8, C.R. 80, 27.   [8] *Instit.* II.12.4, C.R. 30, 342.

11

by the eternal decree of God.'[1] But it is not enough for Calvin to say that God only as the Son is in Christ. So completely is the work of Christ the work of the triune God that he goes further, in commenting on the passage 'God was in Christ reconciling the world to Himself': 'It is also of the Father that this is said, for it would be an improper expression were you to understand it as meaning that the divine nature of Christ was in Him. The Father, therefore, was in the Son in accordance with that statement, "I am in the Father and the Father in me" (John 10.38). Therefore, he that has the Son has the Father also.'[2] The incarnate Son, Jesus Christ, then, is the full and complete revelation of God. 'God is wholly found in Him, so that he who is not contented with Christ alone desires something better and more excellent than God. The summary is this: God has manifested Himself to us fully and perfectly in Christ.'[3] Again, in Christ, God 'communicates Himself to us wholly',[4] and therefore 'they who imagine God in His naked majesty apart from Christ have an idol in place of God'.[5]

At this point we must stop and take account of the limitations that Calvin imposes on what he has just said. Do we have in Christ a full gift of God to us and a full revelation of the nature of God? Calvin is willing to let these statements stand only in a limited sense, for, he says, 'Christ is not better known to us with respect to His hidden divinity than the Father (!). But He is said to be the clear image of God, because in Him God has fully revealed Himself in so far as God's infinite goodness, wisdom, and power are clearly manifested in Him.'[6] Calvin clearly is holding back, reserving, as it were, some other characteristics of God that apparently are not revealed in Christ. We shall find this reservation playing an important part in Calvin's treatment of the work of Christ, where he will speak of the divine nature resting passively during Christ's suffering and not sharing in the work of Christ's human nature. He says, for example, that 'the divine nature was *in a state of repose*, and did not exert itself at all whenever it was necessary in discharging the office of Mediator, that the human nature should act separately, according to

---

[1] *Instit.* II.12.5, *C.R.* 30, 343-344.
[2] *Comm. in 2 Cor.* 5.19, *C.R.* 78, 71.
[3] *Comm. in Col.* 2.9, *C.R.* 80, 104.   [4] Ibid.
[5] *Comm. in 1 Pet.* 1.2, *C.R.* 83, 210.
[6] *Comm. in Joh.* 14.10, *C.R.* 75, 326.

its peculiar character'.[1] Again, Calvin speaks of the 'divine glory, which at that time (the earthly life of Christ) shone in the Father only, for in (Christ) it was concealed'.[2] This question of the glory of Christ reveals the problem clearly. Calvin refers to the passage where Jesus says that He seeks not His own glory, and says that this must not be referred to Christ as God, but only as man, for as God 'He does all things for His own (glory)'.[3] On this the question must be put: Is it not to His own glory that God incarnate, precisely as God, seeks not His own glory? Is not this the glory of God, so different from human conceptions of glory, that He can abandon His own glory? What is the source of Calvin's idea of glory, yes, and of his idea of divinity, which permits him to say that they were hidden in God's revelation of Himself in Jesus Christ? Has God truly revealed Himself in Jesus or not? Commenting on the crucial passage in Philippians 2, Calvin says: 'Christ, then, before the creation of the world, was in the form of God, because from the beginning He had His glory with the Father, as He says in John 17.5. For in the wisdom of God, prior to assuming our flesh, there was nothing mean or contemptible, but on the contrary a magnificence worthy of God. Being such as He was, He could have shown Himself equal to God without doing wrong to anyone; but *He did not manifest Himself to be what He really was*, nor did He openly assume in the view of men what belonged to Him by right.'[4] If that is Calvin's position, then how does he know what Christ 'really was'? What other source does he have for the true nature of the Son of God, and therefore of God Himself? If this other source be the Resurrection, is it not the resurrection of the Crucified, and therefore in no sense a revelation that is in conflict with the Cross? And finally, what has become of the Christ who is the same yesterday and today and forever? Clearly there is a serious problem at the very heart of Calvin's theology, a failure to carry through consequentially his statement that 'they who imagine God in His naked majesty apart from Christ have an idol in place of God'.[5] At one point he comes to the verge of resolving the problem

[1] *Comm. in Matth.* 24.36, *C.R.* 73, 672: . . . '*quievit divinitas, seque minime exseruit.*'

[2] *Comm. in Matth.* 25.31, *C.R.* 73, 686.   [3] *Instit.* II.14.2, *C.R.* 30, 354.

[4] '*Sed non prae se tulit quod erat, neque palam sumpsit in oculis hominum quod iure suum erat.*' *Comm. in Phil.* 2.6, *C.R.* 80, 25.

[5] *Comm. in 1 Pet.* 1.2, *C.R.* 83, 210.

when he says: 'The Father of Christ is the only true God—that is, He is the one God who formerly promised a Redeemer to the world; but the oneness and the truth of Godhead will be found in Christ, *because* Christ was humbled in order that He might raise us on high. When we have understood this, *then* His divine majesty displays itself, *then* we perceive that He is wholly in the Father and that the Father is known wholly in Him. In short, he who separates Christ from the divinity of the Father does not yet acknowledge Him who is the only true God, but rather invents for himself a strange God.'[1] Magnificent as this passage is, it stands on the edge and not in the centre of Calvin's understanding of the divinity of Christ.

2. THE HUMANITY OF CHRIST

Without ceasing to be the Son of God, God the Son also became a man in Jesus Christ. 'The Son of God began to be a man in such a way that He still continues to be that eternal Word who had no beginning in time.'[2] The assumption of real human nature by the Son, the humanity of Christ, plays a most important role in Calvin's doctrine of Reconciliation, for as we are to see, it is precisely in His humanity that Christ performs His atoning work. In fact, it is for the sake of this work that the assumption of human nature is necessary: 'He put on our nature that He might thus make Himself capable of dying, for as God He was not able to undergo death.'[3] We have seen, in the quotation with which Part I began, that reconciliation required that Christ partake of our nature in order to take our place. Our concern here is to show Calvin's understanding of this human nature of Christ.

In becoming man, the Son of God made Himself the brother of men. 'He has adopted us as brothers', Calvin says,[4] and this brotherhood is due to our common nature.[5] Our whole relationship with Christ depends on this common nature. That is why Calvin takes such pains to emphasize the humanity of Christ: 'He who is the Son of God by nature has provided Himself with

---

[1] *Comm. in Joh.* 17.3, *C.R.* 75, 377.   [2] *Comm. in Joh.* 1.14, *C.R.* 75, 14.
[3] *Comm. in Heb.* 2.14, *C.R.* 83, 32. Cf. *Instit.* II.12.3, *C.R.* 30, 342.
[4] *Instit.* II.12.2, *C.R.* 30, 341.
[5] *Comm. in Heb.* 2.16, *C.R.* 83, 34. 'By saying that He came in the flesh, He means that by putting on flesh He became a real man of the same nature with us, that He might become our brother.' *Comm. in 1 Joh.* 4.2, *C.R.* 83, 349.

a body from our body, flesh from our flesh, bones from our bones, that He might be the same with us.'[1] Thus in Christ we find 'a real man composed of body and soul',[2] which constitute His human nature, clearly to be distinguished from His divine nature as God the Son.[3] But it should be noted that Calvin sees the divine assumption of human nature not as an abstract, metaphysical fact but rather as a personal reality of God's reaching out to men in Christ. 'And indeed, if this were impressed on the hearts of all, that the Son of God holds out to us the hand of a brother, and that we are united to Him by the fellowship of our nature in order that He may raise us to Heaven out of our low condition, who would not prefer to keep to this straight road, instead of wandering in rough side roads?'[4]

When Calvin speaks of the human nature of Christ he means human in the full sense of the word: Christ was a man like other men, and He suffered all the weaknesses to which our nature is subject. 'His goodness, which is never sufficiently celebrated, is conspicuous in that He was not reluctant to assume our infirmities.'[5] 'He chose not only to grow in the body but to make progress in mind', like any other man, the only difference between Him and ourselves being that 'the weaknesses which press upon us by necessity were undertaken by Him voluntarily and of His own accord'.[6] He was liable to 'hunger, thirst, cold, and other infirmities of our nature',[7] in a body that was not by nature immune to corruption.[8] But Calvin pushes further the meaning of the word 'infirmities': 'Some understand by it cold and heat, hunger and other wants of the body, and also contempt, poverty, and other things of this kind, as in many places in the writings of Paul, especially in 2 Cor. 12.10. But their opinion is more correct who include, together with external evils, the feelings of the soul, such as fear, sorrow, the dread of death, and similar things.'[9]

Thus our Mediator has drawn near to us in all the weakness of our human condition. 'We have not to go far to seek a Mediator, since Christ of His own accord extends His hand to us; we have no reason to dread the majesty of Christ, since He is our brother;

---

[1] *Instit.* II.12.2, C.R. 30, 341.   [2] *Instit.* II.13.2, C.R. 30, 349.
[3] *Comm. in Rom.* 1.3, C.R. 77, 10.   [4] *Comm. in* 1 *Tim.* 2.5, C.R. 80, 270.
[5] *Instit.* II.16.12, C.R. 30, 378.
[6] *Comm. in Luc.* 2.40, C.R. 73, 104. Cf. *in Matth.* 24.36, C.R. 73, 672.
[7] *Instit.* II.13.1, C.R. 30, 348. Cf. *in Matth.* 21.18, C.R. 73, 584.
[8] *Comm. in Act.* 2.23, C.R. 76, 40.   [9] *Comm. in Heb.* 4.15, C.R. 83, 54.

nor is there cause to fear lest He, as one unacquainted with evils, should not be touched by any feeling of humanity so as to bring us help, since He took upon Him our infirmities in order that He might be more ready to aid us.'[1] No matter how miserable our condition, we are always within the realm of existence that God has made His own in Christ.[2] Not that God needed to do this in order to be merciful; rather, the Incarnation is the revelation to us of the God who is for us. 'The Son of God had no need of experience in order to know the emotions of mercy, but we could not be persuaded that He is merciful and ready to help us had He not been tried by our miseries. But this, as other things, is a gift to us.'[3]

There is, however, a difference between the humanity of Christ and ours: the New Testament 'expressly distinguishes Him from the common condition of mankind, so that He is a real man, and yet free from all fault and corruption'.[4] We shall have occasion to consider how Calvin understands the sinlessness of Christ in the context of the work of Christ, in Part II, but we must also speak of it here in the context of the humanity of Christ. That is not to say that for Calvin the sinlessness of Christ is primarily a condition of nature. If it is also that, it is in the first place a dynamic relationship of the incarnate Son to the Father. In a word, Calvin understands the sinlessness of Christ primarily as obedience.[5] The difference between Christ and ourselves is that the feelings or passions of the soul that are rebellious in us are in Christ obedient to the will of God. 'When God created man, He implanted in him affections, but affections which were obedient and submissive to reason. That those affections are now disorderly and rebellious is an accidental fault. Now, Christ took upon Him human affections, but without disorder; for he who obeys the passions of the flesh is not obedient to God. Christ was indeed troubled and greatly agitated, but in such a way that He kept himself in subjection to the will of the Father.'[6] Calvin emphasizes that Christ assumed voluntarily the weaknesses of our nature in making Himself subject to fear and sorrow and

---

[1] *Comm. in Heb.* 4.15, *C.R.* 83, 54. Cf. *in Heb.* 5.2, *C.R.* 83, 58; *in Col.* 2.18, *C.R.* 80, 111.

[2] *Comm. in Heb.* 4.15, *C.R.* 83, 55.   [3] *Comm. in Heb.* 2.17, *C.R.* 83, 34.

[4] *Instit.* II.13.4, *C.R.* 30, 352. Cf. *in Heb.* 4.15, *C.R.* 83, 54.

[5] *Instit.* II.16.5, *C.R.* 30, 370 *seq.*

[6] *Comm. in Joh.* 11.33, *C.R.* 75, 266. Cf. *in Matth.* 26.37, *C.R.* 73, 720.

understands it as an essential part of what it meant for the Son of God to take on human nature. 'In this way we detract nothing from the glory of Christ when we say that it was a voluntary submission by which He was brought to resemble us in the feelings of the soul. . . . And in this way He proved Himself to be our brother, in order to assure us that we have a Mediator who willingly pardons our infirmities, and who is ready to heal what He has experienced Himself.'[1] But this raises a serious problem. Is it because of the infirmities of fear and sorrow and the dread of death that we need pardon? Is not pardon required, rather, for precisely those infirmities in which Christ, according to Calvin, had no share? Certainly Christ entered into the situation of natural man, God's good creature, but has He entered into the situation of fallen man, the sinner who needs reconciliation? Is the obedience of Christ the miraculous obedience of one who was made sin, who precisely *from the place of sinful man* was nevertheless obedient to the Father, or does Calvin not see it rather as almost a status or condition that Christ enjoyed?

It is not surprising to see that Calvin understands σάρξ in a special sense in John 1.14, and does so quite consciously. 'When Scripture speaks of man contemptuously, it calls him *flesh*. Now, though there is such a great distance between the spiritual glory of the Word of God and the rotten filth of our flesh, nevertheless the Son of God submitted to taking upon Himself that flesh, subject to so many miseries. The word *flesh* is not taken here for corrupt nature, as it is often used by Paul, but for mortal man— though it marks contemptuously his frail and perishing nature, as in these and similar passages: "for he remembered that we were flesh" (Ps. 78.39); "all flesh is grass" (Isa. 40.6).'[2] So also where Paul says that Christ came 'in the likeness of sinful flesh', Calvin comments: 'Although the flesh of Christ was stained with no faults, yet to the sight it seemed sinful, inasmuch as He sustained that punishment which was due to our sins.'[3] And where Paul says that Christ was made sin for us, Calvin says: 'It is commonly said that *sin* here denotes an expiatory sacrifice for sin.'[4] As in Calvin's treatment of the divine nature of Christ, so

---

[1] *Comm. in Joh.* 11.33, C.R. 75, 265.
[2] *Comm. in Joh.* 1.14, C.R. 75, 13.14. Cf. *in Col.* 2.11: 'He takes the term *flesh*, as is his custom, to denote corrupt nature.' C.R. 80, 105.
[3] *Comm. in Rom.* 8.3, C.R. 77, 139.   [4] *Comm. in 2 Cor.* 5.21, C.R. 76, 74.

also here in his understanding of the human nature there is a reservation in the involvement of God in the situation of sinful men. It may be asked whether Calvin has been true to the New Testament witness in seeing the matter in this way. If he would leave something in reserve to God, as it were, would it not have been better to speak of the divine *freedom* in which God has acted and continues to act in Jesus Christ? Would it not have been better to leave God this freedom, rather than to speak of a revelation in which God 'does not manifest Himself as He really is', or of a divine nature that is somehow 'in repose' and not fully active in every moment of the existence of Jesus Christ? And so also with respect to the humanity of Christ, would it not have been truer to the biblical witness and also to the more consequential development of his theology to have seen the obedience of Christ as an obedience precisely in the condition of fallen man? We do not raise these questions as an attack upon Calvin—he himself has presented us with the problem—but are led to question his solutions on the basis of that very biblical witness that was authoritative for him.

To return to the presentation of Calvin's teaching: we have seen that in assuming human nature, although not fallen human nature, the Son of God has united us to Himself. 'When he declares that (Christ) is a man, (Paul) does not deny that the Mediator is God, but wishing to point out the bond that unites us with God he mentions the human nature rather than the divine.'[1] Now, since God is dealing with man, as such, in Jesus Christ, He is therefore dealing with all men, and Calvin could say that 'the salvation procured by Christ is common to all mankind, since Christ, the author of salvation, is descended from Adam, the common parent of all'.[2] All men have this human nature in common with Christ; therefore His work is for all men. 'It was by a wonderful purpose of God that Luke presented Christ to us as the son of Adam, whereas Matthew confined Him within the single family of Abraham. For it would be of no advantage to us that Christ was given by the Father as the author of salvation, unless He had been given without discrimination to all in common.'[3] But when Calvin says that Christ is given to all, on

---

[1] *Comm. in* 1 *Tim.* 2.5, *C.R.* 80, 270. Cf. *Instit.* III. 2.24, *C.R.* 30, 418.
[2] *Instit.* II.13.3, *C.R.* 30, 351.
[3] *Comm. in Matth.* 1.1, *C.R.* 73, 57. Cf. *in* 1 *Tim.* 2.5, *C.R.* 80, 270.

the basis of a common human nature, he means *all* in a special
sense of the word. 'The universal term (*all*) ought to be referred
always to classes of men and not to individuals, as if (Paul) had
said that not only Jews but also Gentiles, not only common people
but also princes, were redeemed by the death of Christ.'[1] Once
more we find Calvin holding back from the consequences of his
own exegesis. In fact, the text says 'all', with no 'as if' or any
other reservation, when it occurs in the New Testament,[2] and
the logic of what Calvin has said about Christ as the son of Adam
calls for a direct exegesis here also. But for Calvin there is a
limitation to the union created by God in assuming human
nature: 'flesh alone does not constitute a fraternal union', for
'the children of God are born, not of flesh and blood, but of the
Spirit through faith'.[3] That is, Calvin refuses to accept a mechanical understanding of reconciliation that might be ours simply on
the basis of a biological definition of man. It may well be asked,
however, if he does not thereby threaten all that he has said
about the consequences of the Incarnation of the Son of God, as,
for example, when he says: 'We have confidence that we are
sons of God *because* He who is the Son of God by nature has
provided himself with a body from our body . . . that He might
be the same as us.'[4] His point of course is to establish faith as the
sine qua non of reconciliation: 'The ungodly, by means of their
unbelief, break off and dissolve that relationship of flesh by which
He has united Himself to us and thus make themselves complete
strangers to Him through their own fault.'[5] But in doing this
Calvin is in danger of raising faith to a higher position than its
object—Christ and His work. And he will also be obliged, as we
shall see later, to make Christ only the *possibility* of reconciliation
rather than its reality, a high price to pay for the establishment
of the necessity of faith. Faith, then, constitutes the boundary
within which Calvin maintains that 'our common nature is a
pledge of our fellowship with the Son of God'.[6]

3. THE PERSON OF THE MEDIATOR

The Mediator has two distinct natures united in Himself.
Before turning to the work of this Mediator, there remains to be

---

[1] *Comm. in* 1 *Tim.* 2.5, *C.R.* 80, 270.   [2] 1 Cor. 15.22; Rom. 11.32.
[3] *Instit.* II.13.2, *C.R.* 30, 350.   [4] *Instit.* II.12.2, *C.R.* 30, 341.
[5] *Comm. in Ps.* 22.23, *C.R.* 59, 231-232.   [6] *Instit.* II.12.3, *C.R.* 30, 342.

c

examined Calvin's understanding of the hypostatic union in Christ. The purpose of the Incarnation was to provide a Mediator who could 'appease God and restore us from death to life'.[1] We shall see in Part II that the death of Christ was essential to His work of reconciliation. For this work the two natures were both necessary: the divine, in order to carry out the work that no man could perform; the human, that acting in our place and in our name He might include us with Him in what He accomplished. 'It was no mean part which the Mediator had to perform, namely, to restore us to the divine favour so as, of children of men, to make us children of God, of heirs of Hell to make heirs of the Kingdom of Heaven. Who could accomplish this, unless the Son of God should become also the Son of Man, and thus receive to Himself what belongs to us and transfer to us that which is His?'[2] Hence the necessity for the two natures: 'As it would have been impossible for one who was only God to suffer death, or for one who was only a man to overcome it, He associated the human nature with the divine, that He might submit the weakness of the former to death as an expiation for sins, and that with the power of the latter He might contend with death and obtain a victory on our behalf.'[3]

But in the Incarnation of the Son of God the two natures remain distinct: 'The unity of person does not hinder the two natures from remaining distinct, so that His divinity retains all that is peculiar to itself, and His humanity holds separately whatever belongs to it.'[4] As Calvin understands the matter, there are in Christ 'peculiar attributes of divinity' and of humanity that must not be confused.[5] For example, His pre-existence, His glory in common with the Father, and His co-operating work with the Father are 'incompatible with humanity' and are attributes of His divinity alone. So also His suffering, His role as Servant, and His death are attributes alone of His humanity.[6] Yet that does not mean that we may separate the two natures. 'God certainly has no blood; He does not suffer, nor can He be touched with hands; but since He who was at once the true God and the man Christ was crucified and shed His blood for us, those things which

---

[1] *Instit.* II.12.4, *C.R.* 30, 343.   [2] *Instit.* II.12.2, *C.R.* 30, 341.
[3] *Instit.* II.12.3, *C.R.* 30, 342.
[4] *Comm. in Joh.* 1.14, *C.R.* 75, 14. Cf. *Instit.* II.14.1, *C.R.* 30, 353.
[5] *Instit.* II.14.2, *C.R.* 30, 354.   [6] Ibid.

were performed in His human nature are improperly yet not without reason transferred to His divinity.'[1] Within the unity, however, there is a distinction of order between Christ's divinity and humanity. For example, He is the heir of the Kingdom of Heaven as God's Son, the human nature that He has in common with us being the means whereby He makes us co-heirs with Himself.[2] Christ's divine nature has priority, and from it by way of His humanity we receive His blessings.[3] Christ is our Redeemer in and through His humanity, but only because He is first of all God: 'The power of God made the flesh of Christ to be a living and spiritual temple.'[4] All that Christ has as man He has not from Himself as man, but from God.[5] 'We conclude, therefore, that Christ, as He is God and man, composed of these two natures united but not confounded, is our Lord and the true Son of God even according to His humanity, though not on account of His humanity.'[6]

It is in the unity of the two natures that we are to see the Mediator, and Calvin insists that in the Bible, 'those things which relate to the office of Mediator do not apply simply to His divinity or simply to His human nature'. These include such matters as the power to forgive sins and to bestow salvation.[7] But the way in which Calvin sees this unity is significant. The constantly repeated formula is: He who as man did such and such was at the same time the Son of God. For example, Christ did not suffer 'in His divinity, but the Christ who suffered in the flesh as an abject and despised man was also as God the Lord of Glory'.[8] Calvin understands the passages in the New Testament in which the properties or attributes of one nature are ascribed to the other as cases of 'communication of properties'. He feels that, properly speaking, they are not strictly correct, but they serve to stress how close is the unity of the two natures in the one Jesus Christ. The Scriptures 'attribute to Him, sometimes those things which are applicable only to His humanity, sometimes those things which belong peculiarly to His divinity, and not infrequently those things which comprehend both His natures

---

[1] *Instit.* II.14.2, *C.R.* 30, 354. [2] *Comm. in Heb.* 1.2, *C.R.* 83, 11.
[3] *Instit.* IV.17.9, *C.R.* 30, 1009.
[4] *Comm. in Heb.* 9.11, *C.R.* 83, 110. Cf. *in Joh.* 5.27, *C.R.* 75, 118.
[5] *Comm. in Heb.* 2.11, *C.R.* 83, 28.
[6] *Instit.* II.14.4, *C.R.* 30, 356. [7] *Instit.* II.14.3, *C.R.* 30, 355.
[8] *Instit.* IV.17.30, *C.R.* 30, 1031-1032. Cf. *in 1 Joh.* 1.1, *C.R.* 83, 300.

but are incompatible with either of them alone. And this union
of the two natures in Christ they maintain so carefully that they
sometimes attribute to one what belongs to the other, a mode of
expression which the ancient writers called *communicatio idio-
matum*.'[1]

Although this attribution to one nature of what strictly speaking belongs only to the other is a witness to the unity of the
person of Christ, Calvin takes pains to point out that it is only a
manner of speaking. This becomes especially clear when it is a
question of the work of Christ. 'Though God and man are united
in one person, it does not follow that the human nature received
what was peculiar to the divine nature; but, so far as was necessary for our salvation, the Son of God kept His divine power
concealed. What Irenaeus says, that His divine nature was
quiescent when He suffered, I understand to refer, not only to
bodily death, but also to that amazing distress and agony of soul
which drew from Him that complaint, "My God, why have you
forsaken me?" '[2] The reservations that Calvin made in dealing
with the divinity of Christ have their consequences in the union
of the two natures in Christ. Or rather, those reservations now
require that he hold separate the two natures in the very climax
of the event of reconciliation on the Cross. The distinction of
natures has become a distinction in the work of Christ, a division
of labour, as it were. Once more we must raise questions. What
is the source of Calvin's knowledge, and of that of Irenaeus before
him, of human nature and of divinity that allows him to measure
Christ and assign part of His work to this nature and part of it
to that? Is not the humiliation of Christ the humiliation of God
Himself? And is it not at the same time the glory of God, a glory
that is so great that it can afford to make itself small? And is not the
humiliation of the Son of God in assuming human nature at the
same time the glorification of man, now raised up into obedient
union with God in Jesus Christ? Again, let it be said that Calvin
himself leads us to ask these questions. He has said that the work of
the Mediator is the work of the two natures in one person. But is
not this the work of the Mediator: that God humbled Himself to
take the place of sinful man and to live the life of obedience in
our place, so that in this one man God is dealing with us all,

---

[1] *Instit.* II.14.1, *C.R.* 30, 353. Cf. *in Act.* 20.28, *C.R.* 76, 469.
[2] *Comm. in Luc.* 2.40, *C.R.* 73, 104.

taking upon Himself the judgment pronounced on us, and exalting us in Christ to a new life in fellowship with God? How then can there be any division of labour in this event of reconciliation?

At one point Calvin comes close to maintaining such a unity in the work of Christ, where, commenting on the exaltation of Christ in Philippians 2.10, he says that this 'is affirmed with reference to Christ's entire person, seen as God manifested in the flesh. For He did not abase Himself either as to His humanity alone or as to His divinity alone, but inasmuch as clothed in our flesh He concealed Himself under its infirmity. So again, God exalted His own Son in the same flesh in which He had lived in the world abject and despised to the highest rank of honour, that He may sit at His right hand.'[1] Yet even here the question may be asked: Is not Jesus Christ the same yesterday and today and forever? Has He not revealed humility to be His glory? And is not man glorified in the very assumption of human nature, prior to the Resurrection? We have seen Calvin reaching back as far as Irenaeus in support of his Christology. If Calvin's Christology reveals problems, they are the problems that he has inherited from the history of Christian dogma, whose difficulties are revealed in Calvin's theology because of his efforts to submit his teaching to the biblical witness.

[1] *Comm. in Phil.* 2.10, *C.R.* 80, 29.

PART II

THE ATONEMENT:
CHRIST IN OUR PLACE

CHAPTER III

THE OBEDIENCE OF CHRIST

1. The Incarnation as Obedience

FOR Calvin there is a direct correspondence between man's deplorable situation and God's saving action. The previous chapters have shown that Calvin insists that our salvation depended upon the Incarnation. But the Incarnation is never separated from its purpose. The cause of the Incarnation was the Fall of man; its purpose is to provide a remedy for the resulting disorder. Calvin no more than begins, therefore, to speak of the Incarnation[1] before going on to speak of the work of Christ by which reconciliation was accomplished. Reconciliation required, he says, 'that man, who had ruined himself by his disobedience, should remedy his condition by obedience, should satisfy the justice of God and suffer the punishment for his sins. Our Lord, then, made His appearance as a real man; He put on the character of Adam and assumed his name, to act as his Substitute in his obedience to the Father, to lay down our flesh as the price of satisfaction to the justice of God, and to suffer in the same flesh the punishment which we had deserved.'[2] We have already seen how Calvin understands the first part of this compact statement of his doctrine of the Atonement: the need for, and the fact of, Christ's assumption of human nature. We turn now to his treatment of the work that Christ performed in our flesh for our salvation.

The first aspect under which Calvin sees that work is that of obedience to the Father. It should be made clear, first of all, that for Calvin obedience is not simply one virtue among others. Obedience to God and to His Word is the source, 'not only of an absolutely perfect and complete faith, but of all right knowledge of God'.[3] Again, the worship that is owed to God by men 'consists

[1] *Instit.* II.12.1-3, *C.R.* 30, 340 *seq.*   [2] *Instit.* II.12.3, *C.R.* 30, 341-342.
[3] *Instit.* I.6.2, *C.R.* 30, 54.

27

solely in obedience'.[1] Obedience is all the more necessary because of the condition of fallen man, for he is no longer able to define his proper duty with respect to God, but must rely upon submission to God's will as revealed in Holy Scripture.[2] It was for the purpose of bringing the whole disordered world back into that order which exists only within the condition of obedience that Christ came into the world.[3] The title of Servant, therefore, 'belongs to all the godly, because they have been adopted on the condition that they devote themselves and their whole lives in obedience to Him'.[4] It must be added that Calvin does not mean to imply that works done in obedience have any value in themselves. What God wants of man is not the static obedience of robots but the dynamic and personal obedience of His children. If He offers rewards for obedience, He does so out of His love and not because our actions have the power to extract an automatic payment. Such actions derive their virtue, 'not from their own dignity or intrinsic merit, but because God values so highly our obedience towards Him'.[5]

Since God's will for men is obedience, and since the fearful situation of man has arisen from his disobedience, Calvin's first answer to the question of how Christ 'has destroyed the enmity between God and ourselves' is 'that He has accomplished this for us by the whole course of His obedience'.[6] Calvin sees the obedience of Christ in three areas of his work: His Incarnation, His earthly life, and His death. We shall examine these in order, beginning with the Incarnation.

The Incarnation of the Son of God is, as Calvin sees it, the first act of the obedience that found its consummation on the Cross, for the Incarnation and the Atonement made by Christ are but two inseparable parts of the one work of Christ. Calvin expresses this in the rhetorical question, 'But has He obeyed in any other way than in the assumed form of a servant?'[7] And again, 'It

---

[1] *Instit.* II.8.5, *C.R.* 30, 270.

[2] *Instit.* II.2.25, *C.R.* 30, 206; I.6.2, *C.R.* 30, 54.

[3] *Comm. in Isa.* 42.1, *C.R.* 65, 59-60.   [4] *Comm. in Isa.* 42.1, *C.R.* 65, 58.

[5] *Instit.* IV.10.15, *C.R.* 30, 878. Cf. III.11.20, *C.R.* 30, 549-550. In order to clarify Calvin's teaching and to show his place in the history of Christian theology, we will compare him in this central part of our study on a number of points with some of the mediaeval theologians. Anselm's teaching on obedience is similar to Calvin's, for he calls it the '*solus et totus honor quem debemus Deo, et quem a nobis exigit Deus*'. *Cur Deus Homo* I.11.

[6] *Instit.* II.16.5, *C.R.* 30, 370-371.   [7] *Instit.* III.11.9, *C.R.* 30, 540-541.

was necessary that He should assume flesh in order that He might submit to obedience.'[1] That is, in order to put Himself in the position of obedience, the Son of God made that first submission to the will of the Father in which He took on human nature. The Incarnation was the foundation of obedience, whereby the Son of God humbled Himself to take the form of a servant, in order to redress the results of the disobedience of man by His obedience in man's place.[2]

2. THE LIFE OF OBEDIENCE

The second part of the obedience of Christ is His whole life on earth or, as Calvin calls it, 'the time of His humiliation'.[3] This is the period in which Christ lived out the perfect obedience of the Servant of God, a title that belongs supremely to Him,[4] so that the cause of our forgiveness is based on 'the whole life of Christ'.[5] Because obedience alone could remedy the ruin caused by the disobedience of man, and because Christ did in fact come into the world 'to surrender Himself in obedience to the Father',[6] Calvin is able to say that 'from the time of His assuming the character of a servant, He began to pay the price of our deliverance in order to redeem us'.[7]

In his commentaries, particularly those on the Gospels, Calvin traces the course of this obedience in the life of Jesus. The key thought in these passages is that of subjection. Christ subjected Himself to His earthly parents, not out of necessity, but because He 'had assumed the character both of a man and of a servant', and this subjection was involved in that higher obedience to God in which He took this humility upon Himself.[8] Further, 'He Himself affirmed that even His baptism completed a part of His righteousness, because He acted in obedience to the command of the Father'.[9] Even His 'paying tribute of His own accord' is cited as a case in which Christ 'declared His subjection, as He had taken upon Him the form of a servant'.[10] The tears shed

---

[1] *Comm. in Isa.* 42.1, C.R. 65, 58.   [2] *Comm. in Phil.* 2.8, C.R. 80, 27.
[3] *Instit.* II.11.12, C.R. 30, 338.   [4] *Comm. in Isa.* 42.1, C.R. 65, 58.
[5] *Instit.* II.16.5, C.R. 30, 371.   [6] *Comm. in Joh.* 10.18, C.R. 75, 246.
[7] *Instit.* II.16.5, C.R. 30, 371.   [8] *Comm. in Luc.* 2.51, C.R. 73, 107.
[9] *Instit.* II.16.5, C.R. 30, 371. Cf. *Comm. in Matth.* 3.13, where Calvin re-states the meaning of Christ's answer to John: 'It is not for us to question which of us deserves to be placed above the other; but rather we should consider what our calling demands, and what is required of us by God the Father.' C.R. 73, 125.   [10] *Comm. in Matth.* 17.24, C.R. 73, 521.

over Jerusalem arose from this same source: 'As there was nothing that Christ wanted more than to carry out the office that had been committed to Him by the Father, and as He knew that the purpose of His calling was to gather the sheep of the lost house of Israel, He wanted His coming to bring salvation to all.'[1] The obedience of Christ was not a cold, blind submission, but rather a fervent desire to carry out the will of the living God.

The will of God is not, however, an indefinite concept for Calvin. At least to the extent that it is right and necessary for us to know the divine will, it is revealed in the Scriptures.[2] Obedience to the will of God, therefore, means obedience to the Word of God, which includes the Law.[3] The fact that man is in revolt against the Law and cannot obey it, and that he is under its curse of death, does not alter the fact that it remains the measure of the 'perfection of righteousness', obedience to which is rewarded by eternal life.[4] Christ, therefore, was made under the Law (Gal. 4.4), which Calvin translates *redactum sub legem* in order to 'express the sense more simply. Christ, the Son of God, then, became subject to the Law, though exempt by right from every kind of subjection. Why? He did so in our name, that He might obtain freedom for us. For just as a man who was free redeems a slave by making himself a surety, and frees the other by putting the chains on himself, so Christ chose to become liable to keep the Law, that we might obtain exemption. Otherwise, it would have been to no purpose that He should have come under the yoke of the Law, for it was certainly not for His own sake that He did so.'[5] Christ's final celebration of the Passover belongs also to this obedience to the Law: 'Having determined to be subject to the Law, that He might deliver us from its yoke, He did not forget this subjection at this last moment.'[6] During the whole course of His life in our flesh, He fulfilled the 'exact righteousness of the Law'.[7] This is the perfect righteousness of Christ, the righteousness of obedience.

But this righteousness of Christ is not regarded by Calvin as existing for itself. 'For what purpose had that submission to the

[1] *Comm. in Luc.* 19.41, *C.R.* 73, 575.
[2] *Instit.* I.6.2, *C.R.* 30, 54; I.13.21, *C.R.* 30, 107; III.21.1, *C.R.* 30, 680.
[3] *Instit.* II.8.5, *C.R.* 30, 269.   [4] *Instit.* II.8.2, 4, 5, *C.R.* 30, 267-269.
[5] *Comm. in Gal.* 4.4, *C.R.* 78, 227.
[6] *Comm. in Matth.* 26.17, *C.R.* 73, 699.
[7] *Comm. in Rom.* 3.31, *C.R.* 77, 67.

Law, but to procure righteousness for us by undertaking to perform that which we were not able to do?'[1] In Part I we have seen that we were incapable of obedience. Here we have seen that Christ was perfectly obedient. The question remains of how Calvin understands this righteousness of Christ's to have been procured for us. The passage cited from the *Commentary on the Epistle to the Galatians* in the previous paragraph provides the clearest answer. The setting is forensic: we owed obedience and could not pay it. Christ put Himself in the position of being able to represent us. He became a man, that He might be the righteous man in our place, putting us to one side, as it were, and taking over the responsibility of performing our work and paying our debt.

Calvin's exegesis of the temptation in the wilderness is important in this connection.[2] The difficulty in this story, as he sees it, is not that Jesus should be subject to temptation, for that is the lot of man, and Christ 'was made man on the condition that, along with our flesh, He should take upon Him our feelings'. Rather, the problem is how He could be tempted and still remain sinless.[3] Calvin's answer may be broken down into three parts: he reminds us first that 'the uncorrupted nature of Adam, while it was still pure and reflected the divine image, was liable to temptation'. Then he says that 'it is rightly considered a weakness of human nature that our senses are moved by external objects; but this would not be sinful in itself, were it not for corruption'. His point is that Christ was able to share the weakness of our nature; yet, being uncorrupted by sin, such weakness was not sinful in Him, since He kept Himself obedient to the Father. But Calvin concludes: 'Christ was separated from us in this respect by the innocence of His nature; though we must not imagine Him to have existed in that kind of condition which was Adam's, to whom it was only given, that it was possible for him not to sin. We know that Christ was fortified with such power that the darts of Satan could not pierce Him.' The last part of this answer throws light on the substitutionary element

[1] *Instit.* II.17.5, C.R. 30, 390.
[2] *Comm. in Matth.* 4.1, C.R. 73, 128 *seq.*, esp. 130.
[3] Cf. *Instit.* II.16.12: Some 'maintain that what is in itself bad may not worthily be attributed to Christ, as though they were wiser than the Spirit of God, who connects these two things together, that Christ was tempted in all things just as we are, yet without sin'. C.R. 30, 378.

of Christ's obedience, as Calvin understands it. Our Substitute has put Himself in our place, and He is able to do so on the basis of a human nature that He has in common with us. Yet has not Calvin endangered this basis by suggesting that between Christ, as man, and Adam (not to speak of sinful man) there is a difference of 'kind of condition'? Surely the obedience of Christ is to be understood as something more than a reflection in His assumed humanity of the perfection of the Son of God. The question here is whether the sinlessness of Christ is to be understood ontologically—in terms of 'condition' or dynamically—in terms of the downward motion of self-humiliation and obedience on the part of God the Son.

The right of Christ to stand in our place, however, rests not only upon His humanity, but also upon the fact that He was sent by the Father for this purpose. Since He is innocent, He has no charge against Himself, and since He became a man, He has the right to stand in our place. To return to Calvin's analogy in the passage from the *Commentary on Galatians*, Christ has come and is in the position to take our place in our chains and to stand as our surety. It should be pointed out here, anticipating what will be said later, that there is a conditional note in this thought. There is no automatic exchange between Christ and ourselves. He was obedient in our place, but that obedience is not *ipso facto* ours. Substitution means, for Calvin, only the possibility that this obedience might be ours. What must take place before it becomes actuality will be the subject of Part III, where we shall see in a new perspective the meaning of the oft-recurring phrase, 'in our place'. Yet at this point we must raise a fundamental question: Is the work of Christ to be understood as having gained the *reality* of salvation, or only as having opened up its *possibility*? If Christ was truly our Substitute and was obedient in our place, ought it not to be maintained that His obedience is already ours, that it was ours while we were yet in our sins, that it stands as God's righteous decision upon us, which we can only accept in faith with thanksgiving? Does not Calvin stand on the same side of this question as Thomas Aquinas, who also saw Christ as the 'cause of universal forgiveness of sins', but added that still 'it is necessary that it be applied' to us individually (by means of baptism and penance and 'the other Sacraments')?[1] An argument

[1] *S.T.* III, *qu.* 49, *art.* 1.

may be raised against an interpretation of Calvin that sees Christ as having gained only the possibility of our salvation, the reality of which awaits a further action of God the Spirit. That argument turns upon the eschatological dimension of Calvin's thought. If this dimension in Calvin's theology is stressed, it might be argued that Calvin sees Christ as the reality of salvation in the sense that He is the one, sufficient foundation of salvation for all men, and that the particular application of this reality in the life of any one man rests, as we shall see later, upon factors not unrelated to Christ, which are not perfectly revealed to faith and which will be manifest only with the final revelation of Christ. Be that as it may, we have raised the question in the sharp form of possibility versus reality, not from a desire to resolve a tension that Calvin saw in the biblical witness, but only to draw attention to a problem that is raised along with this tension, perhaps a problem which must remain unresolved so long as we see only 'through a glass darkly'.

A related problem is raised by Calvin's answer to the question he poses in his *Geneva Catechism* of 1545: 'Why do you pass from the birth (of Christ) directly to His death, omitting the whole story of His life?' His answer is: 'Because only those matters are dealt with here that belong peculiarly to our redemption in such a way that they contain in themselves, in a certain manner, its substance.'[1] Does that mean that Calvin regarded the life of Christ from His birth to His passion as something that does not belong to the substance of our redemption?[2] Certainly in the passages we have quoted the life of Christ is not cut off from His birth and death in such an apparently arbitrary fashion. The solution to this problem must be the one that Calvin himself gives in the *Institutes* of 1559: 'Therefore, in what is called the Apostle's Creed there is very properly an immediate transition from the birth of Christ to His death and Resurrection, in which the sum of perfect salvation consists. Yet there is no exclusion of the rest of the obedience which He performed in his life, just as Paul

---

[1] *Catechismus Ecclesiae Genevensis*, 1545, c. 8, § 55: '*Cur a natalibus protinus ad mortem, omissa totius vitae historia, transsilis?—Quia hic non tractantur, nisi quae redemptionis nostrae ita sunt propria, ut eius substantiam quodammodo in se contineant.*' C.R. 34, 26. The French version of the answer is: '*Pource qu'il n'est icy parlé que de ce qui est proprement de la substance de nostre redemption.*' C.R. 34, 25.

[2] Cf. Barth, K., *Dogmatik in Grundriss*, Zürich, 1947, p. 119.

includes the whole of it, from the beginning to the end when he says that He emptied Himself and took on the form of a servant, and became obedient to the Father unto death, even the death of the Cross (Phil. 2.7).'[1] For Calvin, the whole of the life of Christ stands under the sign of His death, so that a summary of the work of Christ may speak only of His death, for that includes under it His life on earth. 'It may be said . . . that His whole life was nothing but a kind of perpetual Cross.'[2]

3. THE DEATH OF OBEDIENCE

We come now to the principal act of the work of Christ, His death, to be considered under the aspect of obedience. Calvin's main point here is that 'His voluntary submission is the principal circumstance even in (His death), for the sacrifice, unless freely offered, would have been of no use at all in acquiring righteousness.'[3] The life of Christ is not excluded, 'yet, more precisely to define the means of our salvation, the Bible ascribes this in a special way to the death of Christ'.[4] Why is this so? Calvin's answer is that Christ's death was the final proof of His absolute obedience to the will of the Father. And because this obedience was a dynamic response of the human will of the incarnate Son, the final act of submission was not 'without conflict, for He had taken our infirmities also, and it was necessary to give this proof of obedience to His Father'.[5] The important thing to notice here is that the death of Christ is not separated from the reality of the Incarnation and the reality of Christ's human nature. It is to be seen, therefore, not simply as obedience, but as obedience in our place.

The meaning of obedience unto death in Calvin's thought is best seen in his exegesis of the Gethsemane scene and the related passage in Hebrews 5.7ff. There is no attempt in this exegesis to avoid the fact of Christ's fear of death, or of His actual struggle to overcome that fear by faith, in order to remain obedient to His Father in this final temptation in which Christ was confronted by death.[6] Here, at least, there is no suggestion, like that in the comments on the Temptation story, that Christ overcame the

---

[1] *Instit.* II.16.5, *C.R.* 30, 371.   [2] *Instit.* III.8.1, *C.R.* 30, 515.
[3] *Instit.* II.16.5, *C.R.* 30, 371.
[4] Ibid.   [5] Ibid.
[6] *Comm. in Matth.* 26.29, *C.R.* 73, 723. Cf. *in Ps.* 22.16, *C.R.* 59, 228; *in Joh.* 12.27, *C.R.* 75, 291; *Instit.* II.16.11, *C.R.* 30, 377.

fear of death because of a sin-proof nature, superior to Adam's. Instead, the conflict is faced frankly, and Calvin's position here is clearly that Christ overcame that fear by an act of obedient faith,[1] submitting His will to that of the Father, and that not without a struggle.[2] Here, then, is the real difference for Calvin between the man Jesus Christ and ourselves: 'When God created man, He placed in him feelings, but feelings which were compliant and subject to reason. That they are now disorderly and rebellious is an accidental fault. Now Christ took upon Him human feelings, but without disorder, for he who obeys the passions of the flesh is not obedient to God. Christ was indeed troubled and vehemently moved, but in such a way that He kept Himself in subjection to the Father.'[3] The emphasis is not on a difference of ontological condition between Christ and Adam, but on a difference of obedience. But man after the Fall, and as a result of his first act of disobedience, is not able to be obedient.[4] Christ was able to be, and was, perfectly obedient, but the question already raised about the basis of the sinlessness of Christ is not thereby removed. Here also, though in a subtler form, there remains a difference of condition lying behind Christ's obedience and our disobedience. Aquinas had also maintained that Christ had kept His passions subject to reason (*S. T.* III, *qu.* 15, *art.* 4), and Calvin seems to agree. The question remains, however, whether this ordering of the passions is to be regarded as an ontological distinction between Christ's condition and ours.[5] If so, is not the sinlessness of Christ an ontological condition that

[1] *Comm. in Heb.* 2.13: 'He would have had no need of trust, had He not been a man exposed to human necessity. . . . The trust which we put in God, therefore, is an evidence of our helplessness. At the same time, we differ from Christ in this: the weakness which necessarily belongs to us He undertook willingly.' *C.R.* 83, 30.

[2] *Comm. in Heb.* 5.7: 'Christ did not submit to death and the rest of the tribulations because He ignored them or was not pressed down by any feeling of distress, for He prayed with tears, by which He testified to the extreme anguish of His soul.' *C.R.* 83, 62. By contrast, Peter Lombard placed the cause of Christ's sorrow in the 'defection of Peter and the other apostles', as well as in His realization of the scandal that His death would cause. *Sent.* III, *dist.* 15,4.

[3] *Comm. in Joh.* 11.33, *C.R.* 75, 266.

[4] *Instit.* II.2, *passim*, *C.R.* 30, 186 *seq.*

[5] Such an ontological difference is clearly expressed by Anselm, in words all too similar to Calvin's comments on the Temptation story: 'If Adam would not have died if he had not sinned, how much more will He not have to suffer death *in quo peccatum esse non poterit, quia Deus erit?*' *Cur Deus Homo* I.10.

D

endangers the basis of substitution? In what way may this form of obedience be considered as obedience in the place of those whose condition is other than Christ's? To put the question in its most serious form: To what extent has God really entered into the place of *sinful* man to be his Substitute and to save him?

To return to Calvin's teaching, the final significance of obedience is seen only in the actual death of Christ, although Calvin includes in that last measure of obedience the last hours of suffering before the end.[1] In fact, the final agony of Christ is the ultimate proof of His Sonship, for therein is His perfect obedience realized. 'The wicked demand from Christ such a proof of His power that, by proving Himself to be the Son of God, He must cease to be the Son of God. He had clothed Himself with human flesh and descended into the world on this condition, that He might reconcile men to God the Father by the sacrifice of His death. Therefore, in order to prove Himself to be the Son of God, it was necessary that He should hang on the Cross. And now those wicked men refuse to recognize the Redeemer as the Son of God, unless, by coming down from the Cross, He disobey the command of His Father and the order to make expiation for sins and divest Himself of the office divinely appointed to Him.'[2] Not some sign of sheer power is the mark of the Son of God, but a voluntary obedience unto death. His final cry, 'My God, my God, why hast thou forsaken me?', reveals the struggle for obedience, for, faced with dreadful death under the wrath of God, His faith remained, so that still He called upon God. 'While he complained of being forsaken, He still relied on the aid of God as at hand.'[3]

Although death was the final proof of Christ's obedience, it was also the means by which He learned the real meaning of the obedience which He had undertaken. In the act of dying, Christ learned obedience. Commenting on this text from Hebrews, Calvin says: 'The proximate end of Christ's suffering was to accustom Him to obedience; not that He was driven to this by force, or that He had need of such exercise—as do wild oxen or horses when being tamed—for He was more than willing to pay His Father the obedience He owed. But this was an instance and

---

[1] *Comm. in Matth.* 27.34, *C.R.* 73, 765.
[2] *Comm. in Matth.* 27.40, *C.R.* 73, 770.
[3] *Comm. in Matth.* 27.46, *C.R.* 73, 779.

an example of His subjection even unto death. At the same time, it may be said truly that by His death Christ learned fully what it is to obey God, since He was led then to deny Himself completely; for, renouncing His own will, He gave Himself up to His Father so far, that of His own accord and willingly He underwent that death which He dreaded so much.'[1] Here Christ 'became the cause of salvation, because He obtained righteousness for us before God, having removed the disobedience of Adam by the remedy of its opposite'.[2]

We may call Christ's death an act of absolute obedience, according to Calvin, because it was both willed by the Father and undertaken voluntarily by Christ. Calvin takes pains to point out that Christ was in no way forced to do what He did, but acted in complete freedom, giving Himself willingly to the work for which He had been sent.[3] But he also stresses the biblical witness to the fact that it was the Father who willed the suffering and death of His only-begotten Son, that the Cross is the expression of the Father's eternal will.[4] Therefore, the work of the Son conformed to the will of the Father and was that act of perfect obedience required to restore those who were lost as a result of the disobedience of Adam: 'It is God who appointed His Son to be the Propitiator, and who willed that the sins of the world should be expiated by His death. In order to accomplish this He permitted Satan to treat Him with scorn for a short time, as if he were the victor over Him. Christ does not resist Satan in order that He may obey the decree of His Father and may thus offer his obedience as the ransom of our righteousness.'[5] Thus the unity of the Father and the Son in the work of Christ is ensured, in Calvin's theology, not by any form of monothelitism, but by the obedience of Christ, His obedience even unto the death of the Cross.[6]

---

[1] *Comm. in Heb.* 5.8, C.R. 83, 63.   [2] *Comm. in Heb.* 5.9, C.R. 83, 64.

[3] *Instit.* II.16.5, C.R. 30, 371; *Comm. in Matth.* 26.1, C.R. 73, 692; *in Matth.* 26.36, C.R. 73, 719; *in Joh.* 18.4, C.R. 75, 392; *in Joh.* 10.18, C.R. 75, 246.

[4] *Instit.* I.18.4, C.R. 30, 174; *Comm. in Matth.* 26.24, C.R. 73, 702; *in Joh.* 3.16, C.R. 75, 64.

[5] *Comm. in Joh.* 14.31, C.R. 75, 338. Cf. *in Joh.* 6.38: 'Christ declares that He has been manifested in the world in order that He may ratify effectually what the Father has decreed concerning our salvation.' C.R. 75, 146.

[6] Anselm, in the context of his own theology, also sees obedience as the primary note in the relationship of Christ to the Father: 'God did not force Christ to die, for in Him there was no sin, but He (Christ) voluntarily endured

4. As the Work of Christ's Human Nature

We cannot speak of the obedience of Christ in Calvin's theology without speaking of the strong emphasis he puts on the idea that this obedience was performed in Christ's human nature only. Calvin tells us that when the Scriptures call Christ the 'Servant of the Father', or say that 'He does not His own will', these are to be understood as characteristics belonging solely to His humanity.[1] His obedience is therefore to be seen as the work of His human nature,[2] just as the suffering and death that resulted from that obedience were attributes of His humanity alone, for 'God has no blood, nor does He suffer, nor can He be touched with hands'.[3] How, then, does Calvin mean the phrase, 'obedience in our place'? God in the *persona* of the eternal Son has become a man; nevertheless, He has submitted Himself to obedience, not in His divinity, but only in His humanity. That which is in our place and which performs the act of obedience is the humanity of Christ, not the Son of God as such, although Calvin points out that 'the same person, who by reconciling us to the Father in His flesh has given us righteousness, is the eternal Word of God'.[4] And again, 'Certainly when he says that the Lord of Glory was crucified (1 Cor. 2.8), Paul does not mean that He suffered anything in His divinity, but that Christ, who suffered in the flesh as an abject and despised man, was also, as God, the Lord of Glory.'[5] Our assurance that God was involved in the work of Christ would appear to be based on the unity of the two natures in Christ.

But even if this is so, what is the character of this unity of the two natures when Calvin is speaking of the work of Christ? We have seen that Calvin's answer is that the divine nature was *hidden* behind the human, or that it *rested* while the human

death, not in order to abandon life through obedience, but by means of obedience to preserve righteousness, in which He persevered so greatly that He even incurred death.' *Cur Deus Homo* I.9.

[1] *Instit.* II.14.2, C.R. 30, 354. Cf. *Comm. in Isa.* 42.1, C.R. 65, 58.

[2] *Comm. in Isa.* 53.11, C.R. 65, 265.

[3] *Instit.* II.14.2, C.R. 30, 354. Here Calvin stands with the Scholastic theology of the Middle Ages. Anselm had also insisted that the divine nature was not in any way '*posse a sua celsitudine humiliari*'. *Cur Deus Homo* I.8. Lombard exempts the divine nature from all suffering (*Sent.* III, *dist.* 21.2), and Aquinas, speaking of the priestly work of Christ, says: 'Of course Christ was not a priest as God, but as man. Nevertheless, He is one and the same who was priest and God.' *S.T.* III, *qu.* 22, *art.* 3. Cf. *qu.* 46, *art.* 12.

[4] *Instit.* III.11.8, C.R. 30, 538.   [5] *Instit.* IV.17.30, C.R. 30, 1031-1032.

nature was at work: 'We know that in Christ the two natures were united into one person in such a way that each retained its own properties. Specifically, the divine nature rested and did not exert itself at all whenever it was necessary in discharging the office of Mediator that the human nature should act separately according to its peculiar character.'[1] True, Christ could not have performed His work nor have been perfectly obedient if He had not been also God, 'because the power of the flesh was unequal to so great a burden; yet it is certain that He performed all these things *secundum humanum naturam*'.[2] Although it may be that for Calvin Christ 'is in our flesh which he assumed, the only-begotten Son of God',[3] the question remains as to the complete involvement of God in the substitutionary work of Christ. Although Calvin can say that the divine nature of Christ was necessary to His work, that refers to the power of overcoming death, not to His work of humiliation. But should it not be maintained that precisely in Christ's humiliation, in His obedience and in His suffering and death, not the human nature alone was at work, the divinity resting inactive, but also God in His way of being as the eternal Son was at work as our Substitute in our place? In short, are we to try to understand the work of Christ under the presupposition of impassable divinity, or are we to learn first from the Cross what sort of a God was at work in the life of Jesus Christ? Be that as it may, the answer as to the involvement of God in the substitutionary work of Christ, as Calvin understands it, is, not that God Himself in His divinity became our Substitute, but that He who in His humanity entered into our place was at the same time the Son of God. And further, since the work of our Substitute was done in perfect obedience to the will of the Father, there can be no doubt that for Calvin the work of Christ in His human nature is the work of God Himself.

[1] *Comm. in Matth.* 24.36, C.R. 73, 672. Cf. *in Phil.* 2.7, C.R. 80, 26; *in Luc.* 2.40, C.R. 73, 104; *in Luc.* 19.41, C.R. 73, 576; *Instit.* II.14.3, C.R. 30, 355. The same idea is to be found in Lombard: 'Christ died by the recession of His divinity', that is, by its not exercising the effect of its power. *Sent.* III, *dist.* 21.1. The idea that Christ is Mediator only in His humanity is not new in Calvin. Cf. *Sent.* III, *dist.* 19.7; and in Aquinas: *S.T.* III, *qu.* 26, *art.* 2.

[2] *Instit.* III.11.9, C.R. 30, 539. Cf. *in Isa.* 42.1, C.R. 65, 58. Cf. Aquinas: '*Humanitas Christi est divinitatis instrumentum.*' *S.T.* III, *qu.* 48, *art.* 6.

[3] *Instit.* II.14.7, C.R. 30, 359.

CHAPTER IV

SUSTAINED OUR CHARACTER

1. CHRIST AS SINNER

NOTHING could be further from Calvin's meaning than a theory of the work of Christ that spoke only of His obedience and innocence and tried to present the Cross as the conflict of perfect goodness with the evil of the world. On the contrary, Calvin insists that all the circumstances of the life of Christ, especially those of His passion and death, show us that He was sustaining 'the character of a sinner and not of a righteous and innocent person. For He died, not for His innocence, but on account of sin.'[1] We have already considered from the point of view of obedience Calvin's teaching that Christ 'put on the character of Adam and assumed his name to act as his substitute in his obedience to the Father'.[2] Here we must clarify what is meant by such phrases as 'put on the character of Adam' and 'to assume or sustain the character of a sinner'.

The humiliation of the Son of God in taking on human flesh went further than His simply becoming a man. His emptying of Himself led Christ not only to become one of us, but also to descend to the lowest level to which man can sink. His rude birth in a stable was a sign of this,[3] and His final entry into Jerusalem showed that He belonged among the lowest of the people, 'for there can be no doubt that the common people's way of riding is contrasted with royal splendour'.[4] Our attention is drawn to the fact that Christ during the whole of His life 'was abased in His outward appearance and brought down to nothing in the estimation of men; for He wore the form of a servant and put on our nature on this condition: that He be a servant of the Father and even of men'.[5]

---

[1] *Instit.* II.16.5, *C.R.* 30, 372.   [2] *Instit.* II.12.3, *C.R.* 30, 341.
[3] *Comm. in Luc.* 2.7, *C.R.* 73, 73.   [4] *Comm. in Matth.* 21.5, *C.R.* 73, 573-574.
[5] *Comm. in Phil.* 2.7, *C.R.* 80, 26.

To become the lowest of men, however, involves assuming that character of man which makes him the miserable creature that he is. It is not human poverty or social inferiority that separates us from God, but sin, which calls forth God's wrath and judgment. We have seen that Calvin understands the obedience of Christ as a substitutionary action, whereby the Son of God comes to us and puts Himself in the position of being able to become a surety for us and to take our place in the prisoner's dock before the judgment seat of God. But the conditional or potential character of this act must give way to actuality if this substitution is to be effective for our redemption. This further step was made, as Calvin sees it, when Christ 'assumed in a manner our person, that He might be the prisoner in our name, and might be judged as a sinner, not for His own offences, but for those of others (for He Himself was pure and exempt from every fault), and undergo the punishment that was due, not to Himself, but to us'.[1] In a word, Christ in our place means Christ as a sinner.

Christ's assumption of our character as a sinner is carried out by Calvin to its extreme: Jesus must be finally placed between two thieves, 'as if He were the prince of thieves', not because He is that, but because He had taken our place.[2] 'The reason, therefore, for the weakness, pains, and shame of Christ is that He bore our infirmities.'[3] Because Christ became a sinner in our place, 'it is not at all unusual for our offences to be transferred inaccurately to Christ' in the Bible.[4] That is, the reality of Christ's substitution of Himself as a sinner in our place is such that in a manner we may ascribe our sins to Him. Nor is this substitution confined to any one moment of Christ's life. 'Coming into the world to empty Himself and take on the form of a servant, He became a worm and no man, a reproach of men and despised by the people (Ps. 22.7); and finally, He submitted to the accursed death of the Cross. Therefore, He did not refuse to admit . . . disgrace into his genealogy, arising from incestuous intercourse

---

[1] *Comm. in 2 Cor.* 5.21, *C.R.* 78, 74.

[2] *Comm. in Matth.* 27.38, *C.R.* 73, 768. Aquinas gives a number of interpretations of Christ's death between the thieves. One is similar to Calvin's (He was crucified with the guilty as if He were himself guilty, thus bearing our curse), but most of them are related to the idea that the Cross is the judgment between those who believe in Christ (the believing thief) and those who do not (the thief who cursed). *S.T.* III, *qu.* 46, *art.* 11.

[3] *Comm. in Isa.* 53.4, *C.R.* 65, 257.   [4] *Comm. in Ps.* 40.8, *C.R.* 59, 412.

that took place among his ancestors.'[1] Again, commenting on the Lukan account of the purification, Calvin says: 'It ought not to seem odd that Christ, who was to be made a curse for us on the Cross, should for our sake take upon Him our uncleanness with respect to guilt, although He was without fault or crime', or that 'the fountain of purity should wish to be considered unclean in order to wash away our stains'.[2]

But it is above all in the trial and death of Christ that we see 'that He sustained the character of a criminal and a malefactor'.[3] Here we see men standing 'accursed before God and men',[4] as Christ took our place to be 'struck by the hand of God' and to appear to be 'a man utterly abandoned'.[5] By His Incarnation, Christ descended 'to be classed with the common order of men', but in His death, 'the Cross brought Him lower than all men'.[6] He became not only a sinner in our place but 'was abased beneath men'[7] and marked by His criminal's death 'as the most wicked of all'.[8] Even the thief and murderer Barabbas was preferable to this man.[9]

2. As Sinner before God

To be a sinner means that one must face the judgment of God. The fact that Christ had taken our character as sinners is what lay behind the agony of Gethsemane, 'for the Son of God had to undertake this struggle, not because He was tried by unbelief, from which come all our fears, but because He sustained in the feelings of the flesh the judgment of God, the terror of which could not have been overcome without a strenuous effort'.[10] This was the inevitable consequence of Christ's taking our place, if it were to be a true substitution and efficacious for our deliverance from the judgment which was due to us. For, as Calvin puts it, 'having assumed our person and taken upon Him our guilt, He had of necessity to stand before the tribunal of God as a sinner'.[11]

[1] *Comm. in Matth.* 1.3, C.R. 73, 60.   [2] *Comm. in Luc.* 2.22, C.R. 73, 87.
[3] *Instit.* II.16.5, C.R. 30, 372.   [4] *Comm. in Joh.* 19.17, C.R. 75, 414.
[5] *Comm. in Luc.* 23.43, C.R. 73, 775.   [6] *Comm. in Heb.* 2.10, C.R. 83, 27.
[7] *Comm. in Ps.* 22.6, C.R. 59, 224.   [8] *Comm. in Isa.* 53.12, C.R. 65, 266.
[9] *Comm. in Matth.* 27.15, C.R. 73, 755. 'Ideo latrone habitus fuit deterior, ut nos aggregaret Dei angelis.' Ibid.   [10] *Comm. in Heb.* 5.7, C.R. 83, 62.
[11] *Comm. in Ps.* 22.2, C.R. 59, 222. Lombard, on the other hand, sees the fear of Christ as a proof given to us of the human character of His soul. He stresses that, although Christ took our punishment, He did not take upon him our guilt. *Sent.* III, *dist.* 15.1. Neither Anselm nor Lombard nor Aquinas

This is the key to the understanding of the agony and fear of Christ in Gethsemane. It was not simply a fear of death as the termination of life, but the fear of death seen for what it truly is: the judgment of God upon sin. 'What a disgrace, . . . what weakness it would be to be so distressed by the fear of an ordinary death as to be in a bloody sweat and incapable of recovering without the presence of angels! What! Does not this prayer which He repeated three times, "Father, if it be possible, let this cup pass from me" (Matt. 26.39), proceeding from an incredible bitterness of soul, show that Christ had a more severe and strenuous conflict than with an ordinary death?'[1] Not the end of life, but the curse of God was the cause of His fear, 'the curse of God which falls upon sinners'.[2] Nor did He face that curse as any other man might have had to—weighed down with only His own sins—but Christ 'had to wrestle with the guilt of *all* iniquities'.[3] Hence His fear and agony; hence His need to set His face *steadfastly* towards Jerusalem: 'For if no dread, no difficulty, no struggle, no anxiety had been present for Him, what need would He have had to set his face "steadfastly"? But as He was neither without feeling nor possessed of a drunken boldness, He must have been affected by the cruel and bitter death and the awful and horrible torment which He knew threatened Him from the rigorous judgment of God.'[4] In fact, for Calvin, fear of death as such had very little to do with the agony of Christ, for the fearful thing about death is not that we must abandon life, but that we must face the judgment of God, which gives rise to a 'horror in which there is greater misfortune than in death itself'.[5] So for Christ 'that inner fear of the conscience, which made Him so afraid that He sweated blood when he presented Himself before

understood the agony in Gethsemane as the consequence of Christ facing the judgment of God in our place. Lombard comes closest to Calvin when he quotes Augustine as saying that in the prayer in Gethsemane we ought to see that Christ was speaking for us, 'lest it be thought that He feared to die. . . . He said this representing our weakness, on behalf of His feeble followers who fear to die; His voice was theirs.' *Sent.* III, *dist.* 15.1. But this is hardly Calvin's point.

   [1] *Instit.* II.16.12, C.R. 30, 379.

   [2] *Comm. in Ps.* 22.2, C.R. 59, 222. Cf. *Instit.* II.16.12, C.R. 30, 379.

   [3] *Comm. in Heb.* 5.7, C.R. 83, 63. Cf. *in Matth.* 26.39, C.R. 73, 724.

   [4] *Comm. in Luc.* 9.53, C.R. 73, 525.

   [5] *Comm. in Act.* 2.24, C.R. 76, 41. Christ prayed 'not that He might be exempted from death, but that He might not be swallowed up by it as a sinner, for He was sustaining our character there'. *Instit.* II.16.11, C.R. 30, 377.

the tribunal of God, brought Him much greater anxiety and dread than all the torments of the flesh'.[1]

This inward agony of the soul belongs together with the physical agony of the Cross as the two sides of the saving work of Christ for us. This is what it had meant all along for the Son of God to descend to become a man and take our place. No other conclusion to His life could have been possible—for it is the conclusion of the life of sinful man—than that He should endure 'a struggle with the sorrows of death, as if an offended God had thrown Him into a labyrinth of evils'.[2] In this connection Calvin calls our attention to the kind of death that Christ had to suffer: 'By dying in this manner He was not only covered with ignominy in the sight of men, but was accursed in the sight of God.'[3] Thus to the last moment of His life Christ stood in our place as a sinner, and never more so than when He died the death accursed by God, the death of the greatest sinner of all.

As Christ came to stand in our place in order to be a sinner and to suffer for us, so He is a sinner *only* as He is in our place. This we must keep in mind, Calvin insists, when we hear that the Son of God is accursed in the sight of His Father, for He remains at all times the beloved Son of God, 'the unspotted Lamb of God, full of blessing and grace'; but at the same time He had 'taken on Himself our character and thus became a sinner and subject to the curse, not in Himself of course, but in us, yet in such a way that He had to do His work in our name. And so He could not be outside of God's grace, yet He endured His wrath. For how could He reconcile the Father to us if He had Him as an enemy and had been detested by Him? Therefore, He obeyed the Father's will in this matter. Again, how could He have freed us from the wrath of God if He had not transferred it from us to Himself? He was wounded for our sins, therefore, and had to deal with God as an angry judge.'[4] Did Christ actually become a sinner? To this question Calvin would answer that we must first of all rephrase the question. To ask about Christ as a sinner, apart from us and simply in Himself, is to ask concerning the sinlessness of Christ. But if the question is put with reference to the work

[1] *Comm. in Act.* 2.24, *C.R.* 76, 41.
[2] *Comm. in Matth.* 27.46, *C.R.* 73, 780.
[3] *Comm. in Phil.* 2.8, *C.R.* 80, 27.
[4] *Comm. in Gal.* 3.13, *C.R.* 78, 210.

of Christ, and therefore with reference to the substitutionary character of Christ, Calvin insists that He stood in our place as a sinner before God and was treated by the Father as a sinner. In Himself he was pure. But He did not come in order to exist in and for Himself, but to take upon Him our character and to be, in our place, a sinner.

3. Condemned as a Sinner

The character of the sinless Christ as a sinner in our place is clarified by Calvin's exegesis of the trial and condemnation before Pilate. The very fact of this trial and condemnation shows us that Christ was sustaining the character of a criminal.[1] But we must not be offended at this humiliation of Christ, Calvin warns us, nor think that this is something foreign to His calling as Mediator and Saviour which could be set aside as unnecessary or unclean. On the contrary, this condemnation is the 'condition' on which Christ 'undertook the office' to which he was called.[2] Seen in its proper context—that is, as condemnation in our place —it offers us 'no ordinary ground for confidence, which is, that Christ was subjected to the condemnation that we had deserved and was reckoned among transgressors, that we, who are transgressors and loaded with crimes, might be presented by Him to the Father as righteous. For we are accounted pure and free from sins before God, because the Lamb, who was pure and free from every stain, has taken our place.'[3]

But if there was to be a substitutionary submission to the condemnation that we deserved, the condemnation itself had to be made openly by a competent authority. 'As Christ came to bear the punishment of our sins, it was proper that He should first be condemned by the mouth of His judge.'[4] Only when we see this concrete condemnation behind us can we have confidence that there remains no second condemnation before us. And the trial shows us the validity of the verdict. The defendant offered no defence, but remained silent, thereby accepting the verdict as a just one. By His silence He pleaded guilty and was 'condemned as guilty *in persona nostra*, though in Himself he was

---

[1] *Instit.* II.16.5, C.R. 30, 372.
[2] *Comm. in Matth.* 27.46, C.R. 73, 780.
[3] *Comm. in Luc.* 22.37, C.R. 73, 717.
[4] *Comm. in Luc.* 23.4, C.R. 73, 752.

pure'.[1] Now although Christ was innocent in Himself, Calvin
insists that we understand that the trial and condemnation were
perfectly just. This Calvin bases on Christ's silence: 'We ought
not to think it strange that Christ does not answer, at least if we
keep in mind what I have said before, that He did not stand
before Pilate to plead His own cause as is the usual procedure of
those who desire to be acquitted, but rather to suffer condemnation; for it was right that He should be condemned, having
assumed our person. This is the reason why He makes no defence.'[2] Not Christ but we are on trial there before Pilate. It is
our sin that is the charge and it is we who are condemned and
have no defence to make. We know this because Christ stood
before Pilate in our place, not only in the character as man but
also in our character as sinful man. Thus 'we ought to recognize
in ourselves the sinfulness of which He bore the guilt and punishment', for He 'offered Himself in our name before the Father,
that by His condemnation we may be set free'.[3] Our guilt was
pronounced there and we were condemned then once for all.
'For the Son of God chose to stand before an earthly judge, and
to receive the sentence of death there, in order that we, being
delivered from condemnation, may not fear to approach freely
the throne of God.'[4] And again, 'The Son of God stood as a
prisoner before a mortal man and there permitted Himself to be
accused and condemned, that we may stand boldly before God.'[5]

On the other hand, Calvin calls our attention to the fact that
in this trial in which Christ was condemned He was also pronounced innocent: 'He suffered, therefore, under Pontius Pilate
after having been accounted one of the wicked by the solemn
sentence of the governor, yet in such a way that He was at the
same time pronounced to be righteous by the same man, who
confessed that he found no cause for accusation (John 18.38).'[6]
The meaning of this verdict of innocence was not that Christ

[1] Comm. in Matth. 27.12, C.R. 73, 752.
[2] Comm. in Joh. 19.19, C.R. 75, 409-410. Anselm could see the justice of
the death of Christ in the sense of an extra, righteous act that the sinless Christ
did not owe to God; but that leaves no place for a judgment upon Christ that
could be righteous, for the substitutionary note is almost non-existent in his
idea of the Atonement. Cf. Cur Deus Homo II.11. There is no trace of a
substitutionary understanding of the trial before Pilate in either Lombard or
Aquinas.   [3] Comm. in Isa. 53.8, C.R. 65, 261.
[4] Comm. in Matth. 27.11, C.R. 73, 751.   [5] Ibid.
[6] Instit. II.16.5, C.R. 30, 372.

should then have been set free, for as we have seen He was justly condemned, since He stood in our place. On the contrary, God forced Pilate, by such means as the dream of his wife, 'to defend the innocence of His Son, not to rescue Him from death, but only to make it clear that He endured that punishment, which He had not deserved, in the place of others'.[1] By a wonderful dispensation of God, not one but two verdicts were given at the trial of Jesus. 'Thus we shall behold Christ displaying the character of a sinner and malefactor, while from the lustre of his innocence it will appear at the same time that He was loaded with the guilt of others rather than His own.'[2] Pilate may have had something else in mind when he washed his hands of this trial and condemnation, Calvin admits, but he feels that it is clear that 'God wished to testify in this manner to the innocence of His Son, that it might be more evident that in Him *our* sins were condemned'.[3]

4. SURETY AND SUBSTITUTION

We have seen that for Calvin the idea of Christ as a sinner is expressed by the picture of Christ as our surety.[4] Calvin takes pains, whenever he speaks of Christ as a sinner, to stress the innocence of His perfect obedience that kept Him 'free from every fault and stain',[5] for it is only because He is Himself pure that we may be assured that He was condemned for sins other than His own—that is, for our sins.[6] His innocence, being necessary to His office as our surety, does not conflict with His role as sinner in our place.[7] But believers must realize that He 'could not have been their Redeemer in any other way than by taking on Himself the shame and disgrace of a wicked man'.[8] To see Christ as other than a sinner, to look away from His substitutionary character as a sinner in our place, is to see something other than the true Christ. Here, directly in His humility, is where we must see the glory of the Son of God, for Christ is the King of Glory, not apart from His role as a sinner in our place to free us from sin and death, but precisely in that role, 'for nothing more lofty or magnificent belongs to a divine king than to restore life

---

[1] *Comm. in Matth.* 27.19, *C.R.* 73, 756. [2] *Instit.* II.16.5, *C.R.* 30, 372.
[3] *Comm. in Matth.* 27.24, *C.R.* 73, 759.
[4] '*In locum sceleratorum sponsorum, vadem.*' *Instit.* II.16.10, *C.R.* 30, 376.
[5] *Instit.* II.16.12, *C.R.* 30, 378.
[6] *Comm. in Matth.* 27.26, *C.R.* 73, 760.
[7] *Comm. in Rom.* 8.3, *C.R.* 77, 139. [8] Ibid.

to the dead'.[1] The humiliation of the Son of God in standing in
our place as a sinner before God and men is in no way a diminua-
tion of His glory, Calvin tells us.[2] 'If it be objected that nothing
could be less glorious than the death of Christ, . . . I reply, that
in that death we behold a magnificent glory which is concealed
from the wicked, for there we recognize that, sins having been
expiated, the world has been reconciled to God, the curse has
been blotted out, and Satan has been overcome.'[3]

Does this mean that Calvin sees the *humiliation* of Christ as
His true glory, and His role as a sinner in our place as a cause for
Christian joy rather than scandal? If he does so, it is only with
serious reservations. Many of the passages that reveal these
reservations speak more directly of the death of Christ, with which
as such we have not yet dealt, than with Christ as a sinner. Yet
it is not out of place to consider these passages here, for the
offence of Christ as a sinner and the offence of the Cross as the
death of a sinner are one problem for Calvin. Paul had said that
he determined to know nothing but Jesus Christ and Him crucified (1 Cor. 2.2). This, Calvin comments, 'is as though he had
said: "The ignominy of the Cross will not prevent me from
looking up to Him from whom salvation comes, or make me
ashamed that all my wisdom is comprehended in Him—in Him,
I say, whom proud men despise and reject on account of the
disgrace of the Cross." Hence the statement must be explained
in this way: "No sort of knowledge was so important to me that I
should desire to know anything but Christ, *crucified though He
was.*" '[4] Is this really what Paul meant? The 'although' (*licet
crucifixum*) that we find here in Calvin seems to indicate that the
scandal of Christ's humiliation remains a problem for him. There
is a tendency to say 'Christ in spite of His Cross'. Thus Calvin
says that in order 'to prevent the offence of the Cross, (God) not
only promises that the death of Christ will be glorious'—that is,
in itself—'but also commends the many honours with which He
had already adorned it'[5]; as though the humiliation of Christ

---

[1] *Comm. in Luc.* 23.43, *C.R.* 73, 775. Cf. *in Ps.* 22.7: 'The fact that the Son
of God suffered Himself to be reduced so far, and even descended to Hell, is so
far from obscuring His celestial glory, that it is rather a bright mirror of His
incomparable grace towards us.' *C.R.* 59, 224.

[2] *Comm. in 1 Tim.* 3.16, *C.R.* 80, 290.

[3] *Comm. in Joh.* 17.1, *C.R.* 75, 375.

[4] *Comm. in 1 Cor.* 2.2, *C.R.* 77, 333.   [5] *Comm. in Joh.* 12.28, *C.R.* 75, 293.

required contrasting ornamentation in order to show us that it was glorious after all! Referring to the supernatural happenings that took place while Christ was on the Cross, Calvin says: 'Although in the death of Christ, the weakness of the flesh concealed the glory of His divinity for a short time, and though the Son of God was disfigured by shame and contempt, and, as Paul says, was emptied, yet the Heavenly Father did not cease to distinguish Him by some marks, and during His lowest humiliation prepared some indications of His future glory, in order to support the minds of the godly against the offence of the Cross.'[1] Clearly, Christ's role as a sinner and His sinner's death remained an offence for Calvin, an offence that called for *contrasting* ornamentation. As Anselm had maintained that no humiliation could happen to God (*Cur Deus Homo* I.8), and as Aquinas had insisted on the impassability of Christ's divinity (*S.R.* III, *qu.* 46, *art.* 12), so Calvin held back from accepting the full implications of the biblical doctrine of the substitutionary character of Christ. Admittedly he has gone far beyond Aquinas and Anselm in this field, but he has not gone so far as to be able to accept the lowest humiliation of God in Jesus Christ as *itself* the glory and the power of God. There remained for Calvin a tension and an offence in the role of surety that Christ accepted. But it must be said that he avoided any docetic attempt to ease this tension. He insists that Christ took our place as sinners in such a way that the validity and efficacy of this substitution must not be doubted. It was our condemnation that He received from Pilate: 'This is our absolution, that the guilt which made us liable to punishment is transferred to the person of the Son of God.'[2]

The efficacy of this substitution is further ensured by the unity of will between the Father and the Son. Christ's willingness, we have seen, is stressed by Calvin, but on the other side he can say that it was the Father who 'destroyed the power of sin, when its curse was transferred to the flesh of Christ'.[3] Since both Christ and the Father willed this, no limitation can be placed on Christ's substitution of Himself in our place to accept our condemnation. All men are condemned in this man, with the consequence that 'we cannot be condemned for our sins, of whose guilt He ab-

---

[1] *Comm. in Matth.* 27.45, *C.R.* 73, 777-778.
[2] *Instit.* II.16.5, *C.R.* 30, 372.
[3] *Instit.* II.16.6, *C.R.* 30, 373.

solved us when He wished them to be imputed to Himself as if they were His own'.[1]

We have already raised the question of whether Christ's work is the reality of our salvation or only the establishment of the possibility of reconciliation. The question recurs here. It may be said, however, that Calvin himself would probably have put the question in a form more like this: In what *way* is Christ the reality of our salvation? If He is indeed our Substitute (as Calvin maintains), who has stood in the place of all men and has taken their guilt and condemnation upon Himself, then by His work we have been reconciled to God *extra nobis*, and when we accept this reconciliation in faith with thanksgiving in the power of His Spirit, we confess that Christ's saving work has its power and reality quite apart from our acceptance of it.

One is tempted to say to this that Calvin's emphasis on the place of faith might be regarded as endangering the *extra nobis* of our salvation. This is to see the problem as the sharp alternative of possibility or reality. Because Calvin argued that our Substitute is Christ in His humanity rather than God in the *persona* of the Son, and because he could never quite say that God took His own punishment upon Himself, there seems to be some Christological ground for raising the problem in this form. If, however, we put the question as Calvin might have preferred it, asking in what way Christ is the reality of our salvation, the answer, as is well known (*Instit.* III.1.1), is that Christ is the reality of our salvation, but that He is this only as we are related to Him by faith. That is to say, the tension arising from the fact that Christ died for all men and the fact that not all believe is left by Calvin as a tension, resolved neither in favour of universalism nor in favour of a limited atonement. When Christ is known by faith and unites us to Himself by the Holy Spirit, He is the reality of our salvation.

[1] *Instit.* IV.17.2, *C.R.* 30, 1003. Cf. Lombard: 'That punishment with which the Church binds penitents is not sufficient unless (!) the punishment of Christ, who paid for us, co-operate with it.' *Sent.* III, *dist.* 19.4.

CHAPTER V

SUSTAINED OUR PUNISHMENT

1. THE PUNISHMENT ALL MEN DESERVE

WE come now to the very centre of the work of Christ, and, therefore, to the heart of His substitution of Himself in our place. We have seen that Christ takes our condemnation for us. Now, if this substitution is to be efficacious, He must go to the gallows in our place, for 'until Christ relieves us by His death, there remains that iniquity which deserves the anger of God and is accursed and condemned in His sight'.[1] The charge that we are worthy of death stands against us until the sentence of death has been carried out. The fact that another has stood before the judge and accepted that sentence does not mean that execution may now be stayed. That would make nonsense of the justice against which we have offended and fail to take the righteousness of God seriously. 'God who is supremely righteous cannot love the iniquity which He sees in us all.'[2] That is why death must be seen as 'the curse of God' and the sign of God's wrath.[3] This becomes clear when we notice the particular form of death that is carried out here, a death that lies under God's curse: the Cross. 'By dying in this way He was not only covered with shame in the sight of men but was also accursed in the sight of God.'[4] In a word Christ 'suffered that death which the wrath of God inflicts on sinners'.[5]

The Cross was the final revelation of the wrath of God against all men, which showed us 'how dreadful is the judgment of God

---

[1] *Instit.* II.16.3, *C.R.* 30, 370.
[2] *Instit.* II.16.3, *C.R.* 30, 369.
[3] *Comm. in Act.* 2.24, *C.R.* 76, 41; *in Heb.* 5.7, *C.R.* 83, 63.
[4] *Comm. in Phil.* 2.8, *C.R.* 80, 27.
[5] *Instit.* II.16.10, *C.R.* 30, 376. Cf. Lombard: 'He is said to have borne our sins in His body on the tree, because by His punishment which He bore on the Cross all *temporal* punishments which have to be paid for sins are remitted in the baptism of the penitent.' *Sent.* III, *dist.* 19.4.

which could not be appeased but by this price',[1] for it must not be forgotten that God's own Son suffered here. 'Indeed, it was an incomparable display of God's wrath that He did not spare even his only-begotten Son and was not appeased in any other way than by that price of expiation.'[2] The very fact that God accepted His own Son as our surety and gave Him up to such a death reveals the magnitude of His wrath against us, for Christ submitted to the Cross in our place. 'Assuredly we are extremely stupid if we do not see clearly in this mirror how greatly God detests sin, and we are worse than stones if we do not tremble at such a judgment as this.'[3] Christ upon the Cross is held up to us as a mirror in which we see God's wrath against us and the punishment that we deserve. 'In this exhibition God has plainly showed us how wretched our condition would be if we had not a Redeemer.'[4] And so 'we ought to recognize within ourselves that sinfulness of which He bore the guilt and punishment, having offered Himself in our name before the Father, that by His condemnation we may be set free'.[5]

As the one who stands in the place of all men, Christ suffered the punishment corresponding to the charge against Him. As in Gethsemane He had stood before the tribunal of God, 'charged with the sins of the whole world',[6] so at the Last Supper He said that He would shed His blood for many, to which Calvin says: 'By the word *many* He does not mean only a part of the world, but the whole human race, for He contrasts *many* with *one*, as if He had said that He will not be the Redeemer of one man only, but will die in order to deliver many from the condemnation of the curse.'[7] The punishment inflicted on Him is the punishment due to all men.[8] Not some sins only were laid on Him, but all the sins of the whole world. Where Isaiah uses the indefinite 'many' in this connection, Calvin takes him to mean 'all', that being a common way of speaking in the Scriptures.[9]

[1] *Comm. in Isa.* 53.10, *C.R.* 65, 263.
[2] *Comm. in Matth.* 27.45, *C.R.* 73, 778.
[3] *Comm. in Joh.* 19.17, *C.R.* 75, 414.
[4] *Comm. in Matth.* 27.39, *C.R.* 73, 769.
[5] *Comm. in Isa.* 53.8, *C.R.* 65, 261.
[6] *Comm. in Matth.* 26.39, *C.R.* 73, 724.
[7] *Comm. in Marc.* 14.24, *C.R.* 73, 711. Cf. *in Heb.* 9.28, *C.R.* 83, 120.
[8] *Comm. in Matth.* 24.36: '*Non minus insulsi sunt, quod non agnoscunt Christum ideo carnem nostram induisse, ut debitas peccatis nostris poenas in se susciperet.*' *C.R.* 73, 672.   [9] *Comm. in Isa.* 53.12, *C.R.* 65, 267.

Indeed, the unity of the flesh that we have with Christ is enough to assure us that His work is applicable to all men.[1] This unity is no mere figure of speech for Calvin, for he is able to say that Christ, in dying on the Cross, laid down *'our* flesh'.[2] Not only is this death the punishment we deserve, but it is a punishment which we receive in our own flesh, so closely has Christ united Himself with us by standing as our Substitute. Here the idea of substitution is carried through with such thoroughness that it approaches the idea of identity. That is why Calvin says that Christ completed His union with us 'by His death, for by giving Himself for us, He suffered not otherwise than in our person'.[3] 'Christ clothed Himself with our flesh for the purpose of enduring the punishment due to our sins.'[4] In fulfilling this mission He suffered in that flesh which He had put on. Or, to put it in other words, since Christ became that man who is under the curse and subject to death, when He died, that man died. As the Substitute for all men, He received their punishment; at the same time they received that punishment, for His death was accepted as the death of all sinful humanity. God's wrath against men was spent in that our flesh was put to death to endure the punishment that we deserved. Here we see the full implication of the idea of substitution.[5] It would be only a step further to say that to stand in the place of another is to be that other, and to be truly represented by another is to have that other become oneself. But that is to make substitution into complete identity, and Calvin does not do that, for identity means the end of representation. Calvin's idea is substitution, not identity. He does not always press the matter so far as in the passages just referred to, but we must keep these passages in mind in understanding the substitutionary character of Christ's work in Calvin's theology. When Calvin says that Christ suffered 'in our person', and that in dying he laid down 'our flesh', that must be seen as the limit within which he develops his teaching about substitution.

[1] *Instit.* II.12.3, *C.R.* 30, 342.

[2] *Instit.* II.12.3, *C.R.* 30, 341.

[3] *Comm. in Gal.* 2.20, *C.R.* 78, 200.

[4] *Comm. in Matth.* 24.36, *C.R.* 73, 672.

[5] Aquinas would put the emphasis here, not on substitution, but on compensation: the *dignitas* of Christ's person and the greatness of the love out of which He suffered are greater than all sins. Therefore we are freed from punishment by Christ's death. *S.T.* III, *qu.* 48, *art.* 2.

2. CHRIST PUNISHED IN OUR PLACE

In our place and for us Christ suffered the punishment that we had deserved. We have examined this from the aspect of the punishment due to us; now we have to present Calvin's teaching of the substitutionary work itself. The starting point must be to see that Christ's substitution of Himself in our place means not only that He took on the guilt that hung over us and accepted our sentence, but also that He suffered the punishment due to the guilty.[1] 'On this righteous person was inflicted the punishment which was due to us. We could not escape the horrible judgment of God; to deliver us from it, Christ submitted to be condemned even before a wicked and profane mortal.'[2] Condemned in our place, He then took upon Him the whole of the punishment due to man. Man was under the curse; Christ took this curse upon Himself by dying on the Cross, for 'the Cross was accursed not only in the opinion of man, but by the decree of the divine Law'.[3] Commenting on Paul's statement that Christ became a curse for us, Calvin says: 'Christ hung (upon the Cross). Therefore He fell under that curse. But it is certain that He did not suffer that punishment on His own account. It follows, therefore, that either He was crucified in vain, or our curse was laid upon Him in order that we might be delivered from it. And he does not say that Christ was cursed, but, which is still more, that he was *a curse*, for he is pointing out that the curse of *all* men was laid on him.'[4] This is our redemption, not that God's righteousness is simply set aside and our sins overlooked, but that our sins are truly punished, and thus are taken away as a barrier between ourselves and God. 'What is the correction of our peace, but the punishment due to our sins, which we would have had to have paid before we could be reconciled to God, if He had not submitted Himself in our place?'[5] To save us from the punishment that must follow sin, to remove that which separates us from Himself, God sent His only Son to take our punishment in our place. 'In every respect He substituted Himself in our place to pay the price of our redemption. Death held us in bondage under its yoke; Christ, in order to deliver us from it, surrendered Him-

---

[1] *Comm. in* 1 *Pet.* 2.24, *C.R.* 83, 252.   [2] *Instit.* II.16.5, *C.R.* 30, 372.
[3] *Instit.* II.16.6, *C.R.* 30, 373.   [4] *Comm. in Gal.* 3.13, *C.R.* 78, 209-210.
[5] *Instit.* III. 4.30: '*nisi vices nostra ipse subiisset?*' *C.R.* 30, 481.

self to its power in our place. This is what the apostle means
when he writes that He tasted death for every man (Heb. 2.9).'[1]

It should be noted that death, as Calvin sees it, is not a cosmic
force that has control of man, a force that Christ comes to defeat
in order to release us from this foreign captivity. Calvin can use
such language (as in the passage just quoted, where he speaks of
death holding us in bondage), but his quotation from Hebrews,
as well as the preceding sentence, quoted above, shows that he is
thinking of death primarily as the punishment due to sin. Sin
has cosmic consequences,[2] but that is not Calvin's primary concern. His use of such language is only to amplify what he has to
say about death as punishment, the punishment that Christ took
upon Himself. In his commentary on Hebrews 2.9 he explains
this as meaning that 'Christ died for us, for by taking our place
He redeemed us from the curse of death'.[3] Christ's death, therefore, is to be understood personally and substitutionally rather
than cosmologically, the use of cosmological terminology never
replacing the meaning that Christ's work is one of reconciliation
between a loving and righteous God and His sinful creatures.
As 'He fastened to the Cross our curse, our sins, and also the
punishment that was due to us, so He has also fastened to it that
bondage to the Law and everything that tends to bind the conscience. For, on being fastened to the Cross, He took all things to
Himself and even bound them upon Himself, that they might
have no more power over us.'[4] It was our punishment that Christ

---

[1] *Instit.* II.16.7, *C.R.* 39, 374. This substitutionary understanding may be
contrasted with some of the leading mediaeval ideas of the Atonement, where
Christ does not suffer our punishment in our place, but rather in His own place
makes a payment that cancels our debt. Anselm sees Christ's death as that
which was not owed, that which could be freely given, and that which was
worth more than all things under God. This death, therefore, could cancel
out all our debt. *Cur Deus Homo* II.11.14. Lombard maintains that Christ is
able to make a sufficient compensation for our debts by His perfect humility,
qua maior esse non potest. Sent. III, *dist.* 18.5. The Devil and death having tried
to take captive Him over whom they had no right, they must in return grant
us our freedom. *Sent.* III, *dist.* 20.3. Aquinas also has the idea of compensation:
'When a sufficient satisfaction has been produced, the punishment owed is
cancelled.' *S.T.* III, *qu.* 49, *art.* 3. Even when he uses the analogy of a body
—a man paying for the sin committed by his feet with a meritorious action
performed by his hand—the thought is nearer that of compensation than
substitution. *S.T.* III, *qu.* 49, *art.* 3.

[2] *Comm. in Rom.* 8.19: '*Nullum esse elementum nullamque mundi partem, quae non
veluti praesentis miseriae agnitione tacta in spem resurrectionis intenta sit.*' *C.R.* 77,
152.   [3] *Comm. in Heb.* 2.9, *C.R.* 83, 26.   [4] *Comm. in Col.* 2.14, *C.R.* 80, 109.

took upon Him. That is why He wished to be 'judged as a sinner, not for His own offences, but for those of others'.[1] 'He bore the punishment which we would have had to endure, if He had not offered this atonement.'[2]

But if Christ has borne the punishment due to us, that means, Calvin emphasizes, that that punishment now stands behind us. What we had to pay has already been paid in our name. Our debt has been cancelled, not because it was ignored, but because it has been paid in full; the full consequences of our sin have been accepted and dealt with and are no longer ahead of us.[3] The Lamb of God has borne the sins of the whole world. 'The verb *to bear* may be explained in two ways; either that Christ took upon Himself the load with which we were oppressed, as it is said that He carried our sins on the tree (1 Pet. 2.24), and Isaiah says that the chastisement of our peace was laid on Him (Isa. 53.5), or that He blots out sin. But since the latter depends on the former, I gladly accept both, namely, that Christ, by bearing our sins, takes them away.'[4] 'He *sustained* that punishment which was due to our sins.'[5] That means that the punishment which was due to us has been meted out already on the one who volunteered to stand in our place, and who wished to have our sin and guilt charged to Him as our representative, so that we should not have to endure it.

Calvin understands the credal statement that Christ was buried and descended into Hell as a part of Christ's substitutionary submission to our punishment, the omission of which would detract from our understanding of the work of Christ,[6] for 'in His burial the reality of the death which He shared with us is made more clearly apparent'.[7] Calvin sees the burial of Christ as a sign of Christ's substitutionary work, because it attests the reality of this death that should have been ours, and that *is* ours in our representative; although he also sees here the first sign of the glory that was three days later to be Christ's, in that 'His body was not

---

[1] *Comm. in 2 Cor.* 5.21, *C.R.* 78, 74.   [2] *Comm. in Isa.* 53.8, *C.R.* 65, 261.

[3] *Comm. in Isa.* 53.5: '*Christus enim castigationis nostrae, id est, quae nobis debebatur, pretium fuit. Ita pacata est ira Dei, quae in nos merito accensa erat. Pax inita ipso mediatore, qua reconciliati sumus.*' *C.R.* 65, 258.

[4] *Comm. in Joh.* 1.29, *C.R.* 75, 26.   [5] *Comm. in Rom.* 8.3, *C.R.* 77, 139.

[6] *Instit.* II.16.8, *C.R.* 30, 375.

[7] *Comm. in 1 Cor.* 15.3, *C.R.* 77, 538. Cf. *Catech.* c. 9, § 62: '*Atque ut melius patefieret vera morte ipsum defungi, collocari in sepulchro, instar aliorum hominum, voluit.*' *C.R.* 34, 30.

thrown into a ditch in the ordinary way, but honourably laid in a hewn sepulchre'.[1]

But burial as a sign of the reality of death is not as important for Calvin as the descent into Hell, which shows the full content and significance of the death that Christ endured in our place. That our representative should die in our place as a sinner is not enough, for more is due to us than simply death. To set oneself in contradiction to God and His righteous ordering of creation is not so small a thing that it can be settled by mere physical suffering. 'Our ransom also required that He feel the severity of the divine vengeance, in order to appease the wrath of God and satisfy His justice. Hence it was necessary for Him also to contend, with his hands tied, as it were, with the forces of Hell and the horror of eternal death.'[2] Man's rebellion against God is the rebellion of the whole man, body and soul. If that rebel is to be removed, so that God's order may reign unhindered, he must be totally removed. Calvin emphasizes that the descent into Hell, in the sense of being delivered over to the torment and eternal death due to man's soul, was also a part of that substitutionary death that Christ had to endure, for 'He suffered that death which the wrath of God inflicts upon sinners'.[3] 'Not only the body of Christ was given as the price of our redemption, but there was another, greater, and more excellent ransom, for He suffered in his soul the dreadful torments of a damned and lost man.'[4] This is what it means to be a sinner, or rather what it meant for Christ to be a sinner in our place. To submit to God's judgment against the sins of the world means to experience the full consequences of damnation, to be forsaken and abandoned by God.[5]

It would be highly inaccurate to ascribe to Calvin that popular

---

[1] *Comm. in Matth.* 27.57, C.R. 73, 787.   [2] *Instit.* II.16.10, C.R. 30, 376.
[3] Ibid.

[4] *Instit.* II.16.10, C.R. 30, 377. Cf. *Comm. in Matth.* 27.46, C.R. 73, 779. Aquinas gives three reasons for Christ's descent into Hell. The first is similar to Calvin's: Christ came '*poenam nostram portare. Ex peccato autem homo incurrerat non solum mortem corporis, sed etiam descensum ad inferos.*' Therefore, Christ also had to descend into Hell, '*ut nos a descensu ad inferos liberaret*'. He descended, secondly, to free from the Devil those in captivity; and thirdly, to show His power over the dead as well as over the living. *S.T.* III, qu. 52, art. 1. In the next article, however, he maintains that Christ did not descend *ad infernum damnatorum*, but only to that *infernum* where the Holy Fathers waited.

[5] *Comm. in Matth.* 26.37, C.R. 73, 720; *Instit.* II.16.11, C.R. 30, 377.

misconception of the doctrine of the Atonement according to which an angry God exacts the pound of flesh due to Him. If Calvin formulates his doctrine of sin apart from Christology,[1] he also sees sin and the punishment due to it as a reflection of the sentence and punishment that Christ endured in our place.[2] He takes sin seriously, therefore, as he takes the righteousness of God and the conflict between sin and that righteousness seriously. There is a wrath of God, and man has certainly incurred that wrath, but to reduce the doctrine of the Atonement to something so cold and impersonal as the idea of the mere satisfying of an angry God is incompatible with Calvin's teaching. One has only to read his commentary on the mocking of Jesus, for example, to see how far Calvin is from such patterns of thought: 'Our filthiness deserves to be detested by God and warrants that all the angels should spit upon us; but Christ, in order to present us pure and unspotted in the presence of the Father, chose to be spat upon and to be dishonoured by every kind of reproach. For this reason, that disgrace which He once endured on earth obtains favour for us in Heaven and, at the same time, restores the image of God, which had been not only contaminated but almost blotted out by the pollution of sin. Here, too, the inconceivable mercy of God towards us in bringing His only-begotten Son so low on our account shines forth. Also, by this example Christ proved His marvellous love for us, for there was no kind of shame to which He refused to submit for our salvation. But these matters call for secret meditation rather than verbal decoration.'[3]

Christ became our surety before a righteous and loving God, not before a tyrannical despot. But God cannot ignore so serious a matter as our rebellion, for He is righteous and cannot love iniquity.[4] Yet He will not destroy His own creatures, corrupted though they be.[5] Therefore, in His love, God found this way to wipe out sin: in the person of His Son, He came to take our

---

[1] See page 3f.

[2] *Instit.* II.2.20, *C.R.* 30, 201; II.3.6, *C.R.* 30, 215; *Comm. in Isa.* 53.8, *C.R.* 65, 261; *in Joh.* 19.17: '*Nimis certe stupidi sumus, nisi in hoc speculo clare cernimus, quantopere abominetur Deus peccata.*' *C.R.* 75, 414.

[3] *Comm. in Matth.* 27.27, *C.R.* 73, 761.

[4] *Instit.* II.16.3, *C.R.* 30, 369. Cf. Anselm: '*Sic dimittere peccatum, non est aliud quam non punire; et quoniam recte ordinare peccatum sine satisfactione non est nisi punire, si non punitur, inordinatum dimittitur.*' But there is nothing *inordinatum* in God's Kingdom. '*Igitur non decet Deum peccatum sic impunitum dimittere.*' *Cur Deus Homo* I.12.   [5] *Instit.* II.16.3, *C.R.* 30, 369.

punishment in our place. Substitution is the means by which
Calvin sees the wrath and the love of God working together
rather than at cross purposes. In the death of Christ, therefore,
both the wrath and the love of God are revealed.[1] God poured
out His wrath on His Son, whom He loved.[2] This exercise of
God's wrath was not only based on His love for us, that we might
be set free, but is in no way in conflict with the Father's love for
the Son.[3] If we are to understand Calvin's doctrine of the Atonement, we must keep in mind this unity of Father and Son in
God's saving work. And we must remember, further, that the
work of Christ is first of all an act of grace, an action of God's love
to redeem His enemies. He determined on our salvation and
found this way to deliver us from the punishment we had deserved. 'It is no ordinary commendation of grace that God of
His own accord sought out a means by which He might take
away our curse.'[4] This is that love of God for men that must be
seen in the terrible death that Christ suffered, for 'though He was
the well-beloved Son, yet He was not delivered from death until
He had endured the punishment due to us, for it was by that
price that our salvation was purchased.'[5] For Calvin, the death
of Christ is certainly the revelation and the action of God's wrath.
But even more basically, it is the revelation and act of God's love
and grace. 'It is indeed a wonderful goodness of God, and inconceivable to the human mind, that, exercising benevolence
towards men whom He could not but hate, He removed the cause
of the hatred, that nothing might obstruct His love.'[6]

3. REDEMPTION BY SUBSTITUTION

Christ became a sinner in our place to suffer the punishment
that we deserved, and 'took all things to Himself, and even bound
them upon Him, that they might have no more power over us'.[7]

---

[1] *Comm. in Gal.* 3.13, C.R. 78, 210.   [2] *Instit.* II.16.11, C.R. 30, 377.
[3] *Comm. in Heb.* 2.9, C.R. 83, 26-27.
[4] *Comm. in Rom.* 3.25, C.R. 77, 62. Cf. Aquinas: 'To deliver up an innocent
man to suffering and death against his will is unjust and cruel. However, God
the Father delivered up Christ, not in this way, but rather by inspiring in Him
the will to suffer for us. In this is shown both the severity of God, who would
not remit sin without punishment, . . . and His goodness, in that, since man
could not sufficiently make satisfaction by any punishment which he could
suffer, He gave to him a means of satisfaction.' *S.T.* III, *qu.* 47, *art.* 3.
[5] *Comm. in Matth.* 27.43, C.R. 73, 772.
[6] *Comm. in Joh.* 17.23, C.R. 75, 389.   [7] *Comm. in Col.* 2.14, C.R. 80, 109.

Calvin means that, because our punishment has been endured, we are freed from having to undergo it, and because our sins have been condemned in Christ and been borne by Him, they have been removed and no longer stand between us and God: 'Our sins are expiated by the death of Christ.'[1] Our guilt has been wiped out, all the punishment due to us has been carried out, and we have the assurance, on the basis of the Cross, that we are reconciled to God.[2] This is the consequence of the fact that Christ 'was made a substitute and a surety in the place of transgressors, and even submitted as a criminal, to sustain and suffer all the punishment which would have been inflicted on them'.[3]

Nothing, therefore, remains to stand against us, for 'not only did He endure an ordinary kind of death, in order to obtain life for us, but along with the Cross He took upon Him our curse, that no uncleanness might remain in us any longer',[4] and by taking our punishment in our place, Christ 'has obliterated our guilt in the sight of God's judgment'.[5] God's wrath no longer stands over us, for Christ has taken our sins and suffered for them.[6] 'Christ is He who has once discharged the punishment due to us, and has freely offered Himself to take our place, that He might deliver us. He, therefore, who would condemn us, after this, must call Christ Himself to death once more.'[7] That is, to charge us once more for our sins is to deny the reality of the work of the Son of God for our redemption. The element of substitution is so basic to Calvin's Christology that he sees such a charge as the denial of Christ's work, rather than of His substitution. When the reality of our forgiveness is doubted, *He* is called to the Cross again.

By the substitutionary work of Christ we receive redemption. But Calvin wishes there to be no evasion here, and so, following Chapter 16 of the second book of his *Institutes*, which ends with a final summary of the conviction that 'the whole of our salvation, and also each part of it, is comprehended in Christ',[8] when we

---

[1] *Comm. in Rom.* 4.25, C.R. 77, 87.   [2] *Instit.* III.13.4, C.R. 30, 563.

[3] *Instit.* II.16.10, C.R. 30, 376.

[4] *Comm. in Matth.* 27.26, C.R. 73, 760-761.

[5] *Instit.* III.4.26, C.R. 30, 478; cf. II.16.5, C.R. 30, 372.

[6] *Instit.* II.16.6, C.R. 30, 373. Cf. *Argumentum in Evang. Jesu Christi*, C.R. 73, 1-2.

[7] *Comm. in Rom.* 8.34, C.R. 77, 164. Cf. '*En clare vides, Christum peccatorum poenas sustinuisse, ut nos ab illis eximeret.*' *Instit.* III.4.30, C.R. 30, 481.

[8] *Instit.* II.16.19, C.R. 30, 385.

should expect that Calvin has spoken his last word before passing on to the third book, he adds an extra chapter, in which all that has been said about Christ's work in our place is sharpened by a defence of the claim that 'Christ is correctly and fittingly said to have merited the grace of God and salvation for us'.[1] It is the word 'merit' that he wishes to stress, for it excludes every attempt to make the work of Christ merely instrumental to our salvation. But if Calvin seeks to avoid a separation of the Father and the Son by reducing Christ and His work to the level of instrumentality, he also combats a separation that might arise from placing the merit of Christ in opposition to the judgment of God.[2] The substitutionary work of Christ and the righteousness of God are complementary, not contradictory or competitive, in Calvin's theology. A summary of the argument that Calvin employs here will make this clear, and at the same time reveal the importance for Calvin of the element of substitution.

The misunderstanding that must be avoided is that the substitution of Christ in our place is somehow a trick that is played on God, or, to put it in more refined terms, that our redemption by the work of Christ in our place is a sort of fiction, whereby we are placed under a great 'as though', that is in fact not true. Such an error can arise only if we fail to take absolutely seriously the different elements that surround the Cross: the sin of man, the righteousness of God, the unity of the Father and the Son, and the true Incarnation of the Son of God. Sin must be seen as something so serious that man could not resolve it, but only God Himself. God's righteousness must be measured by His treatment of sin in the person of His Son. The unity of Father and Son must be measured by the perfect obedience of Christ, and the Incarnation must be taken seriously as a complete action, whereby Christ became a real man, like ourselves in all things, excepting sin.

We have seen that, according to Calvin, God, in the person of the Son, came down from Heaven and became a man in order to be our Substitute. We have traced out the work done in this substitutionary capacity, the perfect obedience, the trial and acceptance of condemnation as a sinner, and the endurance of the sinner's death. Now, by the use of the word *merit*, Calvin

---

[1] *Instit.* II.17, title, *C.R.* 30, 386.
[2] *Instit.* II.17.1, *C.R.* 30, 386.

sharpens the meaning of substitution in this work, saying that Christ merited for us the favour of God, and, therefore, our redemption.[1] By His perfect obedience and His fulfilment of the Law, Christ proved His own righteousness. But He acted in our name and in our place. 'If righteousness consists in an observance of the Law, who can deny that Christ merited favour for us, when, by bearing this burden Himself, He reconciled us to God, just as though we were complete observers of the Law ourselves? . . . For what was the purpose of that subjection to the Law, but to procure righteousness for us, by undertaking to perform that which we were not able to do?'[2] This righteousness is ours by 'imputation', Calvin adds, but that does not mean a fiction. It means, rather, a reality of grace. For we must remember who it was that stood in our place and acted for us. This was God the Son, who acts in unity with God the Father as one God. This unity had been stressed in the preceding chapter: 'To remove all occasion of enmity, (God) reconciles us completely to Himself by the expiation exhibited in the death of Christ and abolishes whatever is evil in us, that we, who were before polluted and impure, may appear righteous and holy in His sight.'[3] And again: 'The goodness and the infinite love of God towards man appeared in Christ who was given as Redeemer.'[4] So we hear this same unity stressed here: 'The merit of Christ depends solely on the grace of God, which appointed this method of salvation for us.'[5] For Calvin, therefore, 'the death of Christ was the pledge of God's love towards us'.[6] This transaction cannot be a fiction before God, for it was God Himself who put it into action, out of His love for us. By the use of the word *merit*, Calvin tells us that the substitutionary work of Christ being counted as our work is in itself the righteousness of God, in which He is righteous and we are made righteous. That is why Calvin can say that the mercy of God, whereby He forgives us our sins, is to be seen only in the righteousness of God, whereby our sins are punished. God's righteousness is not contrary to God's mercy; it *is* His mercy: 'For in no other way do we know the free mercy of God,

---

[1] *Instit.* II.17.3, 5, *C.R.* 30, 388 and 389.
[2] *Instit.* II.17.5, *C.R.* 30, 390.
[3] *Instit.* II.16.3, *C.R.* 30, 379-380.
[4] *Instit.* II.12.4, *C.R.* 30, 343; cf. *Comm. in Joh.* 17.23, *C.R.* 75, 389.
[5] *Instit.* II.17.1, *C.R.* 30, 387.
[6] *Comm. in Rom.* 5.10, *C.R.* 77, 94.

than if we are persuaded that He spared not His only-begotten Son.'[1]

God has always loved us, but because our sin stood between Him and us, hindering the full exercise of His love and making us subject to His wrath, we are not aware of that love before He reconciles us to Himself in Christ.[2] Although God loved us before the coming of Christ, the work of Christ is not superfluous, for sin had to be wiped out, that we might not be separated from God as sinners under the judgment of death.[3] Christ, therefore, is the means by which our sin is removed, so that we may be fully acceptable to God.[4] Sin can no longer be considered as an obstacle between God and ourselves, for God has already visited His wrath on sin in Christ. In this way, we become recipients of the full love of God. 'Wherefore the beginning of His love is the righteousness described by Paul: "He has made him who did no sin to be sin for us, that we may be the righteousness of God in him" (2 Cor. 5.21). For the meaning is that by the sacrifice of Christ we obtain gratuitous righteousness, so as to be acceptable to God, though by nature we are children of wrath, and alienated from Him by sin.'[5] By Christ's taking our punishment in our place, we, solely by the love and mercy of God who provided this means of salvation, are set free from sin; God has manifested His righteousness, in that sin was condemned, punished, and removed altogether from man's record. But God's righteousness also works our righteousness, for by Christ's substitution we are released from our sins and are made acceptable to God.

'Whence if follows that (Christ) bestows on us what He has obtained, for otherwise it would be improper to ascribe this praise to Him apart from the Father, that grace is His and proceeds

---

[1] *Comm. in Rom.* 5.10, *C.R.* 77, 94. Cf. Aquinas: 'That man should be saved by the suffering of Christ was in conformity with (God's) mercy and with His righteousness. With righteousness, because by His suffering, Christ made satisfaction for the sin of the human race, and *thus* man was saved by the righteousness of Christ. And with mercy, because, since man could not make satisfaction by himself for the sins of the whole human race, . . . God gave His Son as a satisfaction.' *S.T.* III, *qu.* 46, *art.* 1. That is, righteousness and mercy are also united here in the work of Christ. but more in terms of compensation than of substitution.

[2] *Instit.* II.16.3, *C.R.* 30, 369-370; II.17.2, *C.R.* 30, 387.

[3] *Instit.* II.16.3, *C.R.* 30, 369; II.17.3, *C.R.* 30, 388; *Comm. in* 1 *Joh.* 4.10, *C.R.* 83, 354; *in* 2 *Cor.* 5.19, *C.R.* 78, 71-72.

[4] *Instit.* II.17.2, *C.R.* 30, 387-388; II.16.3, *C.R.* 30, 370.

[5] *Instit.* II.17.2, *C.R.* 30, 387.

from Him.'[1] Substitution has two sides. Not only did Christ take from us what was ours, but He had something which He has given to us: His righteousness. Christ did not simply satisfy the demands of God's wrath by submitting to our death. He also lived the life of obedience in our place. Calvin sees the whole life of Christ, not just His death, under the aspect of substitution. We, in the person of Christ, find favour in the sight of God because of His life of humble obedience. We stand before God as righteous men, or, to put it in other words, Christ has procured for us the favour of God.[2] But we can never try to stand before God apart from that substitution. The moment we do so, we are what we were apart from Christ: sinners bound for damnation. Only in accepting Christ Himself as our surety and representative are we accepted before God as righteous, for we are righteous in terms of Christ's righteousness in our place, and not in ourselves. Substitution is the sole basis of our peace with God.

Calvin, following the New Testament, expresses this salvation by substitution in another figure: Christ 'paid the price to redeem us from the sentence of death'.[3] This does not mean that the death of Christ is the price of our redemption in the sense of an equality of payment or value. It expresses, rather, the totality of this exchange. Christ has paid the price in that He has done all that was necessary to redeem us, having borne our punishment, and having performed the obedience for us that God asks.[4] Christ is set in the centre as the substance of our redemption. The grace of God is not to be sought apart from Christ. 'Paul celebrates the grace of God, because he has given the price of our redemption in the death of Christ (Rom. 3.24), and then tells us to flee to His blood, that we may obtain righteousness and stand secure before the judgment of God.'[5]

For Calvin, the work of Christ is not static. The Incarnation and the work of Christ have a purpose. They do not so much

[1] *Instit.* II.17.2, *C.R.* 30, 387-388.

[2] *Instit.* II.17.2, 3, *C.R.* 30, 387, 388. This positive side (as opposed to the negative side of freeing us from punishment) of the work of Christ is seen by Aquinas as taking place in *us*, not in Christ: '*Ad perfectam peccatorum emundationem duo requirentur, secundum quod duo sunt in peccato, scilicet macula culpae, et reatus poenae. Macula quidem culpae deletur per gratiam, qua cor peccatoris in Deum convertitur* (!); *reatus autem poenae totaliter tollitur per hoc quod homo Deo satisfacit.*' *S.T.* III, qu. 22, art. 3.

[3] *Instit.* II.17.5, *C.R.* 30, 389.   [4] Ibid.   [5] Ibid.

establish us in a position as set us in motion. 'Christ suffered in
order to bring us to God. What does this mean, except that we
have been thus consecrated to God by the death of Christ, that
we may live and die unto Him?'[1] By a dynamic and personal
activity, Christ has set us into a dynamic and personal relationship
to God. We are not simply freed from sin, but we are also freed
for life with God. 'Christ offered Himself for us, that He might
redeem us from the bondage of sin, and purchase us to Himself
as property. His grace, therefore, necessarily brings along with
it newness of life, because they who are still slaves to sin make
void the blessing of redemption. But now we are released from
the bondage of sin, in order that we may serve the righteousness
of God.'[2] By the substitutionary work of Christ we have been
redeemed and made righteous before God in order that we might
begin to live the life of righteousness that He lived for us in our
place.

4. THE WORK OF CHRIST AS SACRIFICE

We have examined Calvin's teaching about the work of Christ
in our place in a forensic setting. In doing so we have followed
the main line of Calvin's thought. But there is a secondary
setting which Calvin finds in the Bible, the setting of sacrifice,
priest and sacrificial victim. We must now see whether this
setting affects what we have seen to be central in Calvin's
Christology, the substitutionary character of Christ and His work.

Calvin defends the sacrificial system of the Old Testament from
any suggestion that it was a useless activity. 'God commanded
the sacrifices, not with a design to occupy His worshippers in
terrestrial exercises, but rather that He might elevate their minds
to something higher.'[3] Sacrifice is important as a means of reconciliation, 'for God will never hear us unless He is reconciled;
but first He must be pacified, for our sins cause Him to be displeased with us. Thus, sacrifice must necessarily precede, in
order that there may be benefit from any prayer.'[4] From this
we may learn that 'men are prevented from appearing before
God, for, as He is justly displeased with them all, there is no
reason why they may promise themselves any favour with Him
until He is pacified. There is, moreover, but one way of pacifica-

---

[1] *Comm. in* 1 *Pet.* 3.18, *C.R.* 83, 264.   [2] *Comm. in Tit.* 2.14, *C.R.* 80, 424.
[3] *Instit.* II.7.1, *C.R.* 30, 253.   [4] *Comm. in Heb.* 8.3, *C.R.* 83, 97-98.

tion: an expiation with blood. Hence no pardon of sins can be hoped for unless we bring blood. This is done when we flee by faith to the death of Christ.'[1] The sacrifices of the Old Covenant, important as they are, do not have their importance in themselves, for they were only 'shadows, whose body we have in Christ'.[2] By the sacrifices of the Law, 'the faithful were plainly and openly instructed that salvation was to be sought solely in that expiation which has been accomplished by Christ alone'.[3] That is what gives them their significance and importance: 'that Christ put an end to them by His Advent takes nothing away from their sanctity, but rather commends and illustrates it. For just as they would have presented an empty spectacle to the old people unless the power of the death and Resurrection of Christ had been shown there, so, had they not been brought to an end, it would not be possible today to see why they were instituted.'[4] Thus the whole sacrificial system of the Old Covenant was typical of the work of Christ, in whom it finds its true fulfilment, and therefore its cessation. 'From the Law, therefore, we may learn to know Christ properly, if we consider that the Covenant which God made with the Fathers was founded on the Mediator, that the sanctuary by which God manifested the presence of His grace was consecrated by blood, that the Law itself, with its promises, was ratified by the shedding of blood, that one priest was chosen out of the whole people to stand in the presence of God in the name of them all, not as an ordinary mortal, but clothed in sacred garments, and that no hope of their reconciliation with God was given to men but through the offering of sacrifice.'[5] So, as a true type of what was to be fulfilled in Christ, 'the old tabernacle was not an empty invention of man, but the effigy of the heavenly tabernacle'.[6]

The sacrificial system contained essentially two parts: the priest, and the victim. Both were typical of Christ.[7] 'The Levitical priests were antetypes representing Christ, who, as the Mediator between God and men, was to reconcile the Father to us by His most perfect purity.'[8] Christ having come, 'all the

---

[1] *Comm. in Heb.* 9.22, *C.R.* 83, 116.   [2] *Instit.* II.7.16, *C.R.* 30, 264.
[3] *Instit.* II.6.2, *C.R.* 30, 248.   [4] *Instit.* II.7.16, *C.R.* 30, 264.
[5] *Comm. in Luc.* 24.27, *C.R.* 73, 807.   [6] *Comm. in Heb.* 8.2, *C.R.* 83, 97.
[7] This idea was of course present in scholastic theology. Cf. Aquinas, *S.T.* III, *qu.* 22, *art.* 2, 4; Lombard, *Sent.* III, *dist.* 20.5.
[8] *Instit.* IV.12.25, *C.R.* 30, 922.

priestly offices have been transferred to Christ, having been fulfilled and finished in him; therefore every right and honour of
the priests has been transferred to Him alone'.[1] The word 'alone'
is stressed by Calvin, because Christ was not made one priest
among others, but has a permanent and eternal priesthood, for
'He was consecrated by His Father a priest and a high priest not
for a limited time'; therefore, 'Christ, who is immortal, requires
no vicar to be substituted in His place'.[2]

As the fulfilment of the priestly figure under the Old Covenant,
however, it was necessary that this final and perfect high priest
be able to be the priest of men. 'Hence it follows that it was
necessary for Christ to be a real man, for as we are very far from
God, we stand in a manner before Him in the person of our
priest, which could not be were He not one of us. Hence, that
the Son of God has a nature in common with us is so far from
diminishing His dignity that it commends it the more to us, for
He is fitted to reconcile us to God because He is a man. Therefore, Paul, in order to prove that He is the Mediator, expressly
calls Him man, for had He been taken from among angels or
any other beings, we could not be united by Him to God, as He
could not have reached down to us.'[3] Our priest is one of our
number and acquainted with our infirmities.[4] We must also
know that 'the priest did not minister privately for himself, but
was appointed for the common good of the people. But it is of
great consequence to notice this, so that we may know that the
salvation of us all is put in motion by and revolves on the priesthood of Christ.'[5] Christ came to be a human priest, one who
could stand as our representative before God, whose priestly
activity was for our benefit rather than for His own. The representative character of priesthood means that He acts in our place
in so close a union with us that we are all involved in His work.
'Christ sustains the character of a priest, not only to render the
Father favourable and propitious to us by an eternal law of
reconciliation, but also to associate us with Himself in so great an
honour (Rev. 1.6). For we, who are polluted in ourselves, are
nevertheless priests in Him, and offer ourselves and all that we

[1] *Instit.* III.4.4, *C.R.* 30, 459.
[2] *Instit.* IV.18.2, *C.R.* 30, 1052.
[3] *Comm. in Heb.* 5.1, *C.R.* 83, 57.
[4] *Comm. in Heb.* 5.2, *C.R.* 83, 58.
[5] *Comm. in Heb.* 5.1, *C.R.* 83, 57.

F

have to God.'[1] Thus, Christ's priestly act, because it is a *priestly* act—that is, an act of representation—becomes ours. By making Himself our priest, He takes us up into His act, since He performs it for us in our place. We stand before God in the person of our priest.

In 1 John 2.1-2 Christ is called 'righteous' and a 'propitiation', to which Calvin says: 'It is necessary for Him to be both, that He might sustain the office and person of an Advocate; for who that is a sinner could reconcile God to us? For we are all excluded from access to Him, because no one is pure and free from sin. Hence no one is fit to be a high priest, unless he is innocent and separated from sinners, as it is said in Hebrews 7.26. *Propitiation* is added, because no one is fit to be a high priest without a sacrifice.'[2] This passage is of interest for two reasons. First, it shows that Calvin cannot speak of the office of priest without speaking of his function, which is to offer sacrifice. The person is never separated from the work, the Incarnation from the Atonement, in Calvin's theology. Secondly—and this is of special interest to our investigation—this passage reveals that Calvin can pass from forensic language to sacrificial as though the two terminologies were equivalent, which shows us that, although the figures are different, the basic thought that we have previously followed in a forensic setting remains the same here.

'The Levitical priests were commanded to prefigure the sacrifice which was to be accomplished by Christ.'[3] But there was a great difference between the type and the fulfilment; for Christ did not suffer the defects of the ancient high priests, who had to offer sacrifices for their own sins as well as for the sins of the people, and who had to offer repeated sacrifices.[4] The most striking difference, however, is in the sacrifices that they offered. 'The offering of blood was common to both, but there was a great difference as to the blood, for Christ offered, not the blood of beasts, but His own blood.'[5] Christ, as our high priest, is also the victim. 'To prove that He is the sacrifice for our sins, He wished both to be led out of the city, and to be hanged on a tree, for the

---

[1] *Instit.* II.15.6, *C.R.* 30, 367. Aquinas quotes, but does not develop, a similar passage from Augustine's *de Trinitate:* '*unum in se faceret pro quibus offerebat*'. *S.T.* III, qu. 22, art. 3.
[2] *Comm. in* 1 *Joh.* 2.1, *C.R.* 83, 309.
[3] *Instit.* IV.18.12, *C.R.* 30, 1059.   [4] *Comm. in Heb.* 7.27, *C.R.* 83, 95.
[5] *Comm. in Heb.* 9.11, *C.R.* 83, 109. Cf. *Instit.* IV.14.21, *C.R.* 30, 958.

sacrifices, the blood of which was shed for sin, used to be carried out of the camp, in accordance with the commandment of the Law, and the same Law pronounces a curse upon anyone who hangs on a tree (Lev. 6.30; 16.27; Deut. 21.23). Both were fulfilled in Christ, that we might be fully convinced that our sins have been expiated by the sacrifice of His death.'[1] Christ is Himself the sacrifice offered to take away sin, for what all the sacrifices of the Law prefigured 'was accomplished in Him alone. Now we know that Moses says frequently that an atonement shall be made for iniquity and that the sin shall be blotted out and forgiven. In short, the ancient figures teach us excellently what is the power and efficacy of the death of Christ.'[2]

The presupposition of the argument here is what Calvin calls 'a fundamental principle: that without shedding of blood there is no remission'.[3] But Calvin does not mean simply that we must look to the old practices under the Law, and thereby learn what is the meaning of Christ's death. Certainly, he is interested to show that what happened in the death of Christ was the fulfilment of the sacrificial system, but he can also turn it round, and work from the revelation in the death of Christ back to the true understanding of this claim, that apart from the shedding of blood there is no forgiveness. 'As without Christ there is no purity nor salvation, so nothing without blood can be either pure or saving, for Christ is never to be separated from the sacrifice of His death.'[4] Seen in the light of Christ, the importance of sacrifice in the Old Testament is evident: it is a type of the perfect sacrifice of Christ, by which the sins of the world are taken away.

5. SACRIFICE AS SUBSTITUTION

We have already seen in Calvin's commentary on 1 John 2.1 that he can use the terms 'advocate' and 'high priest' as synonymous titles for Christ, which indicates that he is saying the same thing in both forensic and sacrificial terminology. The central theme of his forensic figure is substitution, and substitution is at the heart of his exposition of the work of Christ in terms of sacrifice. The priest stands for the people, performing his function for them and in their place, just as the surety stood in the place

---

[1] *Comm. in Joh.* 19.17, C.R. 74, 413.   [2] *Instit.* II.17.4, C.R. 30, 388.
[3] Ibid. Cf. *Comm. in Heb.* 9.22, C.R. 83, 116.
[4] *Comm. in Heb.* 9.22, C.R. 83, 116.

of all men in being perfectly obedient to His Father. And as that obedience is seen as ours, because it is performed in our place and in our name, so we stand before God in the person of our priest, and are made priests in Him.[1] Already, therefore, in the person of the priest we find the same characteristic of substitution that appears in the forensic setting.

But the real emphasis on substitution comes in the consideration of the sacrificial victim, for the victim was nothing other than a substitute, under the laws of sacrifice. 'In the Jewish ceremonies there was rather a confession of sin than an expiation of them, for what did they do in offering sacrifices, but confess themselves worthy of death, since they substituted vicarious victims in their own place?'[2] The victim was their substitute to take the punishment that they deserved, and therefore the very act of sacrifice should teach men their own inability to sustain God's wrath, and their need for a representative. 'It was by no means reasonable that an innocent animal should be substituted in the place of a man, to be exposed to the curse of God, except that believers might learn that they were in no wise competent to bear God's judgment, nor could they be delivered from it otherwise than by the transfer of their offence and guilt.'[3] The true 'means of making peace with God was disclosed when Christ, being made a curse, transferred to Himself the sins which alienated men from God (2 Cor. 5.19; Gal. 3.13; Ps. 51.19)'.[4] In fulfilling the priestly office of the Old Covenant, Christ fulfilled the whole of the sacrificial system, by becoming that Substitute for us which was prefigured by the sacrificial victim.

The intimate connection between Christ as priest and Christ as victim is seen in the unity of these two parts under the Law, for the priest had no purpose apart from sacrifice. 'The priest without a sacrifice is no peacemaker between God and man, for without a sacrifice sins are not atoned for, nor is the wrath of God pacified.'[5] The sacrifice of Himself is therefore the primary characteristic of Christ's fulfilment of the old priesthood. 'The principal office of Christ is briefly but clearly stated, which is, that He reconciles men to God, taking away the sins of the world by the sacrifices of His death. There are other benefits indeed,

---

[1] *Comm. in Heb.* 5.1, *C.R.* 83, 57; *Instit.* II.15.6, *C.R.* 30, 367.

[2] *Instit.* II.7.17, *C.R.* 30, 265.   [3] *Comm. in Lev.* 16.20, *C.R.* 52, 504.

[4] Ibid.   [5] *Comm. in Heb.* 5.1, *C.R.* 83, 58.

which Christ confers upon us, but this is the chief one, and the rest depend on it: that, by appeasing the wrath of God, He makes us to be reckoned righteous and pure.'[1] Simply to speak of Christ as priest, therefore, is meaningless, if we do not see that He was a priest only in so far as He offered up a sacrifice for our sins. Without that, His priesthood would be useless. 'In order that our priest may appease the wrath of God, and procure his favour for us, an atoning sacrifice must intervene.'[2] 'Now, as under the Law God commanded victims to be offered to Him from the flock, a new and different method has been adopted in the case of Christ, that the same one who was the priest should be the victim, because it was not possible to find any other adequate satisfaction for sins or anyone worthy of so great an honour as to offer to God His only-begotten Son.'[3]

Christ as sacrificial victim, however, is essentially the same as Christ as surety. By the name alone we may see that the essential character of the victim in the Hebrew sacrificial system was that of a substitute. 'The victims and expiations offered for sins were called אשמות (a word which properly signifies sin itself), by which change of name the Spirit intended to suggest that they, being equivalent to vicarious victims, received and sustained the curse due to sins.'[4] Substitution was also the implicit significance of the act of offering a victim. 'Whenever a victim was sacrificed, did not the people that stood by behold in it a representative of their death? For when men substituted an innocent animal in their place, they confessed that they themselves deserved that death.'[5] The victim stands in the place of the sinner, and suffers his punishment in his place. 'The sacrificial victim was offered so as to expiate sin by enduring its punishment and curse. And this was suggested in the sacrifices by the laying on of hands, as if the sins of the whole people were thrown upon the victim.' In like manner, 'our sins were thrown upon Christ so that He alone bore the curse'.[6] It must of course be remembered that for Calvin the representative character of the sacrifices under the Old Covenant were only typical, and had efficacy only in so far

1 *Comm. in Joh.* 1.29, *C.R.* 75, 25.
2 *Instit.* II.15.6, *C.R.* 30, 366.
3 Ibid. *C.R.* 30, 367.
4 *Instit.* II.16.6, *C.R.* 30, 373. Cf. *in 2 Cor.* 5.21, *C.R.* 78, 74.
5 *Comm. in Col.* 2.14, *C.R.* 80, 108.
6 *Comm. in Isa.* 53.10, *C.R.* 65, 262-263.

as they prefigured the one efficacious sacrifice on the Cross.[1]

If any doubt remains that these two ways of seeing the work of Christ are the same for Calvin and have the same theme of substitution, it may be removed by Calvin's comments on the text from 1 Peter, 'who his own self bore our sins in his body on the tree'. 'This way of speaking,' he says, 'is fitted to express the efficacy of Christ's death. For as under the Law the sinner substituted a victim in his own place, that he might be released from guilt, so Christ took upon Himself the curse due to our sins, that He might blot it out before God. And he adds expressly, *on the tree*, because he could not offer such an expiation except on the Cross. Therefore Peter expresses the truth well, that Christ's death was a sacrifice for the expiation of our sins; for being fixed to the Cross and offering Himself a victim for us, He took on Himself our guilt and our punishment. Isaiah (53.5), from whom Peter has taken the substance of his teaching, employs various forms of expression; that He was struck by God's hand for our sins; that He was wounded for our iniquities; that He was afflicted and broken for our sake; that the chastisement of our peace was laid on Him. But Peter intended to express *the same thing* by these words, even that we were reconciled to God by this means, that Christ made Himself *a surety and a prisoner for us before His tribunal*, that He might suffer the punishment due to us.'[2] Sacrificial victim and surety are but two ways of seeing the work of Christ as substitutionary.

As surety, Christ offered no defence before Pilate; as one sent to be a sacrifice, He said nothing to prevent the completion of His work for us.[3] As our surety, He took our death in our place; as our sacrifice He offered Himself up for us.[4] Calvin can move from one terminology to the other, for both express substitution. Commenting on the text, 'He made him to be sin', he asks, 'What is denoted by *sin*? It is the guilt by which we are bound under the judgment of God. As, however, the curse of a man was cast formerly on the victim, so Christ's condemnation was our absolution, and with His stripes we are healed.'[5] Calvin can

---

[1] *Instit.* II.7.16, *C.R.* 30, 264; II.16.6, *C.R.* 30, 373.

[2] *Comm. in* 1 *Pet.* 2.24, *C.R.* 83, 251-252.

[3] *Comm. in Matth.* 26.62, *C.R.* 73, 738.

[4] *Instit.* IV.18.3, *C.R.* 30, 1053.

[5] *Comm. in* 2 *Cor.* 5.21, *C.R.* 78, 74. According to Aquinas, this passage means that Christ was made *hostiam*, a sacrificial victim for sin, or that He had

also use sacrificial terminology without any special sacrificial meaning, and even when he is using a forensic setting. On Col. 1.22 he says, '(Paul) meant to say, therefore, that the Son of God had put on the same nature with us, that He took upon him this mean, earthly body, subject to many infirmities, that He might be our Mediator. When he adds, *by death*, he again calls us back to sacrifice. For it was necessary that the Son of God should become man and be a partaker of our flesh, that He might be our brother; it was necessary that He should become a sacrifice by dying, that He might make His Father propitious to us.'[1] For *sacrifice* one could perfectly well read *surety*, for the meaning is the same. We have also seen in his comments on 1 John 2.1 that he can use the word *advocate* where the context would lead us to expect him to say *high priest*.[2]

Finally, as Calvin has stressed the total and eternal efficacy of the death of Christ in forensic terms, so he can say the same thing in sacrificial terms. 'Christ, at the moment of His death, declared that by His single sacrifice He had accomplished and fulfilled everything that was necessary to our salvation.'[3] This offering is not to be repeated, for its efficacy is eternal.[4] 'Christ, when He comes, will make it known how truly He has taken away sins.'[5] Thus, 'it is not sufficient to know that Christ is the sole victim, unless we also know that there is only one oblation, that our faith may be fixed upon His Cross'.[6] Here again we are held to the one substitution of Christ in our place, by which our sins and their punishment are removed once and for all. Sacrifice and surety are but two different biblical ways of seeing the substitutionary character of Christ's work.

6. Satisfaction and Substitution

Satisfaction is a word that is often regarded as too hard or too impersonal to use as a description of the atoning work of Christ, yet it is frequently used by Calvin. We have reached a point now from which we may examine his use of this idea, to see what is implied by it, and how it is related to the central theme of

similitudinem carnis peccati, that is, a passable and mortal body. He does not point up any substitutionary significance. *S.T.* III, *qu.* 15, *art.* 1.

[1] *Comm. in Col.* 1.22, *C.R.* 80, 90.

[2] The passage is given on p. 68.

[3] *Instit.* IV.18.3, *C.R.* 30, 1053.

[4] Ibid.

[5] *Comm. in Heb.* 9.28, *C.R.* 83, 120.

[6] *Instit.* IV.18.6, *C.R.* 30, 1056.

substitution. When Calvin says that the 'satisfaction for our sins was accomplished on the Cross',[1] there arises once more the danger of seeing Christ's death as the pound of flesh, the payment of which is necessary to appease an angry God. The connotation for Calvin of God's satisfaction, however, is far from that of a cruel miser who insists on getting what is his due. If we are to understand what he means by the word satisfaction, we must forget all such ideas, and return to the framework of the theology of the Atonement which we have been examining. Calvin speaks of the death of Christ as a satisfaction and that term has its place within the realm of Christ's substitution of Himself in our place. Further, satisfaction is a word which is used with respect to the relation between Christ and His Father, and we have seen that the Father and Son are united in this work of redemption. Whatever else it may mean, satisfaction cannot imply any opposition between Father and Son, for that would be an opposition of God with Himself. Such a misunderstanding is ruled out when we hear such words as these: 'It is God who appointed His Son to be the Propitiator, and who willed that the sins of the world should be expiated by His death.'[2] But Father and Son are united not only in the initiation of the work of Christ. They are also united in its execution, for the Father was not 'a mere spectator' of our salvation, Calvin tells us, but the 'Author of salvation'.[3] And to make Calvin's position perfectly clear: 'The most merciful God, when He determined on our redemption, became *Himself* our Redeemer in the person of his only-begotten Son.'[4] We have already seen, moreover, that the obedience of Christ assures us that His work is the exact will of the Father. But Calvin also insists that the Father was active in this work. 'God was in Christ reconciling the world to Himself' has two meanings, as Calvin sees it. It means that the Father was in Christ, as well as

---

[1] *Comm. in Rom.* 4.25, C.R. 77, 87.

[2] *Comm. in Joh.* 14.31, C.R. 75, 338. Anselm endangers this unity by conceiving of the death of Christ as that which is not owed to God: '*imo necesse esse video, ut Pater Filio retribuat*' (*Cur Deus Homo* II.11.19), although he has before said: '*in una persona totus Deus cui secundum hominum se obtulit, intelligitur*'. Ibid. II.18.

[3] *Instit.* III.22.6, C.R. 30, 692.

[4] *Instit.* I.12.2: '*Sese ergo clementissimus Deus in persona unigeniti Redemptorem nostrum fecit, dum nos redemptos voluit.*' C.R. 30, 341. Contrast Anselm: 'The Father did not will to restore the human race, *nisi faceret homo* (!) *tam magnum aliquid, sicut erat mors illa.*' *Cur Deus Homo* I.9.

the Son. 'Therefore we should learn to be contented with Christ alone, because in Him we also find God the Father, as He truly communicates Himself to us by Him.'[1] An interesting if unfortunate illustration of the extent to which Calvin emphasizes the concern of the Father in the work of Christ is his interpretation of the destruction of Jerusalem as the revenge of God for the death of His Son, showing that God would never have allowed Christ to die, 'unless He had been an expiation for the sins of the world'.[2] But, we must ask, if that was God's intention, why should He take revenge on this part only of that world for which he gave His Son? If He gave his Son *for* the world, how can there be revenge? This talk of revenge strikes a discordant note with the rest of Calvin's teaching, and if it shows the danger of Calvin's reservation in his understanding of God's involvement in the affairs of sinful man, it also reveals his concern to show that the gift of the only-begotten Son was no small matter to God.

If God loved His Son with such a love, we realize how much He loved us, for whose sake He gave Christ over to death.[3] So the New Testament witnesses that 'this was done through the grace of God towards us, through which it was that He did not spare even His own Son'.[4] Thus, 'Christ is so illustrious and singular a proof of the divine love towards us, that whenever we look upon Him, He fully confirms to us the teaching that God is love'.[5] This is the framework within which we must understand Calvin's use of the word *satisfaction*: the unity of the Father and the Son, the love of the Father for the Son, and His love for us that was so great that He gave His Son for our redemption.

What, then, can Calvin mean by the idea of satisfaction? His meaning is the same as when he speaks of Christ's death as 'the payment or compensation which absolves us from guilt'.[6] Satisfaction, like payment, tells us of the absolute character of the work of Christ. Calvin tells us that such strong words are used in the Scriptures and should be used in the Church because they

---

[1] *Comm. in 2 Cor.* 5.19, C.R. 78, 71.

[2] *Comm. in Luc.* 23.28, C.R. 73, 763.

[3] *Instit.* II.16.3, C.R. 30, 369-370; *Comm. in 1 Joh.* 4.10, C.R. 83, 354.

[4] *Comm. in Heb.* 2.9, C.R. 83, 26-27; cf. *Instit.* III.14.17: '*Efficientem enim virae aeternae nobis comparandae causam ubique Scriptura praedicat Patris caelestis misericordiam, et gratuitam erga nos dilectionem.*' C.R. 30, 575. Cf. *Instit.* III.14.21, C.R. 30, 578.

[5] *Comm. in 1 Joh.* 4.9, C.R. 83, 353.   [6] *Instit.* II.17.5, C.R. 30, 389.

show us 'more literally how great was the calamity' from which we have been delivered.[1] No idea of equivalence between the damage caused by sin and the reparation provided by Christ is intended by the words *payment* and *satisfaction*, but, like the word *merit*, they force on our attention the completeness of Christ's work, in which all is done that must be done for our salvation.[2] Only when we realize how much has been done for us can we understand how much had to be done for us.[3] Satisfaction means that the obedient suffering of Christ in our place is completely efficacious and sufficient.

First this word calls our attention to Calvin's teaching that it is Christ and He alone who is the expiation for sins, who reconciles us to the Father, so that we should not seek any other means by which we might be saved than Himself. 'It would not be sufficient to know that God forgives us our sins, unless we came directly to Christ and to that price which He paid on the Cross for us.'[4] 'Where man's highest good exists, there is his glory.'[5] Christians glory therefore only in the Cross of Christ, 'for it is He alone by whom and for whose sake we have God propitious to us'.[6] The true honour due to Christ is that He be considered what He is, the satisfaction for our sins; that is, the perfect surety and sacrifice, sufficient for all the sins of all the world. '(Jesus) did not assert in a few words that the Christ ought to have suffered, but explained at length that He had been sent in order that He might expiate the sins of the world by the sacrifice of His death, that He might become a vicarious victim in order to carry the curse, that by His condemnation He might wash away the filth of others. . . . The sum of what is stated is, that the disciples are wrong to be upset about their Master's death— without which He could not discharge what belonged to the Christ, for His sacrifice was the most important part of redemp-

---

[1] *Instit.* II.16.2, *C.R.* 30, 369.

[2] Calvin's use of the word *satisfaction* is to be distinguished from the idea of equality or compensation that is to be found in Anselm: 'Therefore, know most certainly that without a satisfaction, *i.e.* without the voluntary repayment of what is owed, God is not able to forgive sin unpunished.' *Cur Deus Homo* I.19. And again: '*Secundum mensuram peccati opportet satisfactionem esse.*' I.20. Aquinas says that a satisfaction must make an equal restoration. '*Aequalitas autem in satisfactione ad Deum non est secundum aequivalentiam sed magis secundum acceptionem ipsius.*' *S.T.* III, *Suppl.*, qu. 14, art. 2.

[3] *Instit.* II.3.6, *C.R.* 30. 215.   [4] *Comm. in* 1 *Joh.* 2.12, *C.R.* 83, 316.

[5] *Comm. in Gal.* 6.14, *C.R.* 78, 265.   [6] *Comm. in Col.* 1.20, *C.R.* 80, 88.

tion—for in this way they shut the gate, that He might not enter into His Kingdom. This ought to be carefully observed, for, since Christ is deprived of the honour due to Him if He is not reckoned a sacrifice for sins, the only way by which He could enter into His glory was that humiliation (Phil. 2.7) out of which the Redeemer appeared.'[1] Christ alone is the sufficient means of redemption.[2]

Because that is so, satisfaction also means that all sins have been dealt with in Christ, and that the total man as sinner stood under God's rejection, in Christ's death, so that God's judgment of sin is final in this one act.[3] 'Our salvation is perfectly accomplished in His death, because by it we are reconciled to God, satisfaction is given to His righteous judgment, the curse is removed, and the punishment sustained.'[4] No exception may be made to the completeness of this work. 'To take away sins is to free from guilt those who have sinned by His satisfaction. (Paul) says *many*, for *all*, as in Rom. 5.15. Indeed, it is certain that not all receive the benefits from the death of Christ, but this happens because their unbelief prevents them.'[5] As far as the work of Christ is concerned, however, the punishment for all sin has been sustained, and that means that in His death sinful man has been put to death, so that God will no more deal with us as sinners. This death has the power, therefore, to reconcile us completely to the Father by washing away all our sins.[6] 'Should anyone, under the pretext of the universality of this expression, raise a question with respect to devils, whether Christ be their peacemaker also, I answer, No, nor of ungodly men either, though I confess that there is a difference, for the benefit of redemption is offered to the latter, but not to the former.'[7] The work of Christ

---

[1] *Comm. in Luc.* 24.26, C.R. 73, 80.

[2] Anselm arrives at a similar conclusion, though by a different method: only God can make the required satisfaction, yet man must pay it; thus in the God-man alone is to be found the satisfaction necessary to save men from death. *Cur Deus Homo* II.5.11.

[3] *Comm. in Col.* 1.14, C.R. 80, 84. Cf. *Instit.* II.9.2, C.R. 30, 311; II.11.12, C.R. 30, 338.

[4] *Instit.* II.16.13, C.R. 30, 380.   [5] *Comm. in Heb.* 9.28, C.R. 83, 120.

[6] *Comm. in 1 Joh.* 1.7, C.R. 83, 306. Cf. Anselm: Because the goodness of Christ is greater than the evil of all sins, '*vides igitur, quomodo vita haec vincat omnia peccata, si pro illis detur*'. *Cur Deus Homo* II.14. Aquinas says the suffering of Christ was '*sufficiens et superabundans satisfactio pro peccato et reatu generis humani*'. *S.T.* III, qu. 48, art. 4.

[7] *Comm. in Col.* 1.20, C.R. 80, 89.

is for all men, therefore, and if some will not accept it, that is
their fault, and in no way due to any inadequacy in what Christ
has done. This one act of substitutionary obedience and suffering
is valid, moreover, for all time, even to eternity, 'for though
pardon is to be asked for daily, as we daily provoke God's wrath,
yet, as we are reconciled to God in no other way than by the
guarantee of the unique death of Christ, sin is rightly said to have
been destroyed by it'.[1]

It now becomes clear what satisfaction has to do with substitution: satisfaction is a way of saying what has been accomplished
by substitution. It means that God has nothing more to say to
us as sinners, for as sinners we have died. We exist before God
only as His obedient and righteous servants, not in ourselves, but
in Christ. That Calvin takes the representative character of
Christ as seriously as these words imply is proved by his saying:
'By laying down *our flesh* He has paid the price of satisfaction to
the justice of God.'[2] Satisfaction means that sin had to be and
was removed. Sinful man was tried and convicted, he was put
to death, and he suffered in his flesh the punishment he deserved.
Satisfaction was accomplished by substitution. This is our redemption, and what we have received must never be separated
from the way in which we have received it, which is the death
of Christ in our place.[3]

Satisfaction for our sins, or their expiation, is sometimes seen
by Calvin in connection with the innocence of Christ, as when
he says: 'If the Son of God had not been free from all sin, we
should have had no right to look for expiation from His death.'[4]
The meaning here is that only He who does not deserve death is
free to take the place of those who are condemned and to die in
their place. If He too had had to die for His own sins, He could
not have died for us as well. The innocence of Christ ensures
that His death was in our place, and was therefore a satisfaction
to God's righteous judgment of sin.

[1] *Comm. in Heb.* 9.26, C.R. 83, 119. Cf. *in Heb.* 10.15, C.R. 83, 127; *in
1 Joh.* 4.10, C.R. 83, 354.

[2] *Instit.* II.12.3, C.R. 30, 341.   [3] *Comm. in Eph.* 1.7, C.R. 79, 149-150.

[4] *Comm. in Matth.* 27.26, C.R. 73, 760. It is an important element of
Anselm's doctrine of the Atonement that Christ did not have to die. *Cur Deus
Homo* II.10. Aquinas, while maintaining that Christ had to die, because He
had assumed a mortal body, grounds this necessity in the love out of which
Christ assumed this body. *S.T.* III, *qu.* 14, *art.* 2. So he can say: '*Non enim
satisfactio efficax nisi ex caritate procederet.*' *S.T.* III, *qu.* 14, *art.* 1.

When Calvin says that 'Christ, by His obedience, has satisfied the judgment of the Father',[1] the meaning is that Christ has won for us, by His obedience in our name, the right to be accepted by God, for the work of Christ is not only negative, in the sense of removing our sins, but also positive, in that we become righteous before God. As the judgment of God demands the removal of sin, so it demands the existence of righteous men, and *both* are accomplished by the substitutionary work of Christ. The same obedience that qualified Him to be our Substitute, so that He could take our punishment, also made us, by virtue of that substitution, righteous. 'By enduring the curse of the Cross, He raised up in splendour *our* righteousness as a trophy of victory.'[2] His righteousness is ours, just as His death is ours, because it was performed in our place and in our name. Nor is this righteousness theoretical; it is concrete and real, for the substitution was of such a nature that He acted in our own flesh. It was our flesh that was put to death, our flesh that was given up to its well-deserved punishment. 'Being about to make atonement for sins, He put on our nature that we might have in our own flesh the price of our reconciliation.'[3] That is why Calvin can say that 'in Him our sins were condemned'; our guilt was removed, so that satisfaction having been made, we are free 'to come into the presence of the Heavenly Judge'.[4]

Finally, in understanding the word *satisfaction* within the context of the substitutionary work of Christ, we must remember the dynamic quality of Calvin's theology. The work of Christ is not static, nor is its purpose static. The Cross puts us in motion, not in the sense that the work of Christ is only a beginning that needs to be completed, but in the sense that we are put into a dynamic relationship with God because of our union with Christ. It is not just that our past is put away. A future is placed before us, a future inseparably connected with the substitution that Christ has made of Himself in our place. 'Let us now remember that it was not with reference to Himself alone that Christ committed His soul to the Father, but that He included as it were in one bundle all the souls of those who believe in Him, that they may be preserved along with His own. And further, by this

---

[1] *Comm. in Rom.* 3.24, *C.R.* 77, 61.   [2] *Comm. in Joh.* 6.55, *C.R.* 75, 155.
[3] *Comm. in Heb.* 2.17, *C.R.* 83, 35. Cf. *in Luc.* 22.19, *C.R.* 73, 710; *Instit.* II.12.3, *C.R.* 30, 341.   [4] *Comm. in Matth.* 27.24, *C.R.* 73, 759.

prayer ("Father, into Thy hands I commend my spirit"), He obtained authority to save all souls, so that not only does the Heavenly Father deign for His sake to take them into His custody, but, giving up the authority into His hands, commits them to Him to be preserved."[1] Christ did not die as a single man, alone and to Himself; He died as our representative, so that we are united with Him in His death, because of the union He has made between Himself and ourselves by becoming our true Substitute, and we have therefore died with Him. This is what Calvin calls 'the general end of His death: that we, being dead to sins, might live to righteousness'.[2] But as we died as sinners by the substitutionary death of Christ, so this new life becomes ours by way of the Resurrection of Christ, to which we must now turn.

[1] *Comm. in Matth.* 27.50, *C.R.* 782.
[2] *Comm. in* 1 *Pet.* 2.24, *C.R.* 83, 251.

CHAPTER VI

RESURRECTION AND ASCENSION

1. RELATION OF THE RESURRECTION TO THE DEATH OF CHRIST

CALVIN says that 'the whole accomplishment of our salvation, and all the separate parts of it, are contained in (Christ's) death'.[1] But when he comes to the Resurrection of Christ, he says it is that 'without which what we have said thus far would be mutilated'.[2] Within this apparent contradiction we shall discover more precisely what Calvin means by the substitutionary character of the work of Christ. But first we must see how Calvin understands the relationship between the death of Christ and His Resurrection.

The glory of the Resurrection does not draw us away from the Cross. Commenting on the text in which Paul glories in the Cross of Christ, Calvin says: 'Where man's highest good exists, there is his glory. But why is it not elsewhere? For although salvation is offered us in the Cross of Christ, what about His Resurrection? I answer that in the Cross our whole redemption and all its parts is contained, but the Resurrection of Christ by no means leads us away from the Cross.'[3] Death and resurrection go together inseparably. Calvin advises us to remember in reading Scripture that whenever we find the death of Christ mentioned alone, it includes what belongs to the Resurrection, and *vice versa*.[4] Yet within this unity, the Resurrection has its particular place as the revelation of the glory, the power and the efficacy of the Cross, 'for as He appeared the conqueror of death by rising from the dead, so our faith in that victory rests on His Resurrection alone'.[5] That does not mean that we are to think only on the Resurrection. As we contemplate the work of Christ

---

[1] *Comm. in Joh.* 19.30, C.R. 75, 419.   [2] *Instit.* II.16.13, C.R. 30, 379-380.
[3] *Comm. in Gal.* 6.14, C.R. 78, 265.   [4] *Instit.* II.16.13, C.R. 30, 380.
[5] Ibid.; *Comm. in Act.* 13.30, C.R. 76, 298.

for us, we must start from the Cross and go on to the Resurrection.[1]
The Cross, which in itself looks like failure, is revealed for what
it truly is by Christ's Resurrection.[2]

Although the Cross and Resurrection of Christ belong together,
they have a definite order. The Resurrection is the second
member in an irreversible order. 'In order to know His glory,
it is necessary to proceed from His death to His Resurrection.
Many stumble at His death, as if He had been vanquished and
overwhelmed by it, but we ought to keep in mind His power and
majesty in the Resurrection. On the other hand, if anyone
choose to begin with the Resurrection, he will not follow the
order prescribed by the prophet, nor comprehend the Lord's
strength and power.'[3] For Calvin there is no *theologia gloriae*
that is not at the same time a *theologia crucis*. 'Ministers of the
Word who wish to teach effectually ought always to join the
ignominy of His death to the glory of His Resurrection.'[4] Resurrection is a rising from the dead, and it always 'contains within
it the idea of death'.[5] The Resurrection of Christ not only
accords with His death, therefore, but even confirms it. 'Christ
so rose from the dead that, still, His death was not abolished but
retains its efficacy for ever, as though (the author of Hebrews)
had said: "God raised up His Son, but in such a way that the
blood He shed once for all in his death is efficacious after His
Resurrection for the ratification of the everlasting covenant and
brings forth its fruit just as if it were always flowing." '[6]

The connection between the Crucifixion and the Resurrection
means that the substitutionary work of Christ does not end in
His death. Had death been the end of His work, we, in whose
name He died, would be as dead men in the sight of God, fit only
to be buried and forgotten. But Christ's purpose was our restoration to life with God; therefore, something more besides the
Cross was necessary. This purpose was accomplished when Christ
'obtained the victory over death, to which He submitted in the

[1] *Comm. in Matth.* 26.29: '*Ita videmus, ut manu ducat suos discipulos ad crucem,
et inde in spem resurrectionis eos extollat. Sicut autem illos dirigi ad mortem Christi
oportuit, ut per illam scalam in coelum adscenderent.*' C.R. 73, 709.

[2] *Instit.* II.16.13: '*Sic tamen ut huius (i.e.* of the Cross) *beneficio vim efficaciam-
que suam illa* (the Resurrection) *nobis proferat.*' C.R. 30, 380.

[3] *Comm. in Isa.* 53.3, C.R. 65, 256-257.

[4] *Comm. in Matth.* 16.20, C.R. 73, 479.

[5] *Comm. in Phil.* 3.10, C.R. 80, 50.

[6] *Comm. in Heb.* 13.20, C.R. 83, 197.

weakness of the flesh, not by help obtained by begging, but by the operation of His Heavenly Spirit'.[1]

This insistence on the Resurrection as the work of Christ Himself is to be found in Calvin's early *Commentary on Romans* of 1539. At that time he insisted that 'surely Christ rose by Himself and by His own power; but as He is accustomed to assign to the Father whatever divine power is in Himself, so the apostle, not improperly, has transferred to the Father that which was a most proper work of the divinity in Christ.'[2] Here we must raise two questions: what sort of death would that be from which Christ could deliver Himself? And if He raised Himself by His divine power, what consolation is that for us who have no such power? This conception of the Resurrection seems to endanger the reality of Christ's death as well as our confidence that Christ's Resurrection ensures our own. Whether for this or for other reasons, Calvin seems to have dropped this insistence in his later works, where he speaks instead of the 'power of God' that 'appeared in raising up Christ'.[3] And even more clearly, he says that Christ 'obtained what He wanted when He came forth a conqueror from the pains of death, when He was *sustained by the saving hand of the Father*, when after a short conflict, He won a glorious victory over Satan, sin and Hell'.[4] But in either case, we must remember Calvin's careful preservation of the distinction between the two natures of Christ. Christ died for us in His human nature, the divine nature being at rest. Now we see the full power of that divinity asserting itself in His Resurrection, so that although there was a complete death in our place, He, who was our Substitute in His flesh, was also the Son of God and had power to overcome death. 'For we know that the body of Christ was liable to death, and that it was exempted from corruption, not by its essential property (as it is said), but solely by the providence of God. Therefore, Christ was not only earthly as to the essence of His body, but was also in an earthly condition for a time; for before Christ's power could show itself in conferring the heavenly

---

[1] *Comm. in Rom.* 1.4, C.R. 77, 11.

[2] *Comm. in Rom.* 8.11, C.R. 77, 146. Aquinas also maintains that 'Christ rose by His own power', and he adds that since the divine power and activity of the Father and of the Son is the same, it is the same thing to say that Christ was raised by the power of the Father as that He was raised by His own power. S.T. III, qu. 53, art. 4.

[3] *Comm. in Act.* 13.30, C.R. 76, 298.   [4] *Comm. in Heb.* 5.7, C.R. 83, 63.

G

life, it was necessary that He die in the weakness of the flesh. This heavenly life first appeared in the Resurrection, that He might give life to us also.'[1] Although Christ might have evaded death by His divine power, still 'He died naturally like the rest of men, given over to death, and received immortality in the same flesh which He had assumed in a mortal state'.[2] Certainly Calvin has left no room for a docetic interpretation of the Cross. But he says that in the suffering and death of Christ the divine nature was passive, beginning only in the Resurrection to assert its full power. The complete activity and therefore the complete revelation of God appear, it would seem, only now. But ought we not to recognize the humiliation of Christ also as the complete activity and self-revelation of God? Has not Calvin limited the significance of the Cross by a presupposed concept of impassibility in God?

He who died rose again in the same flesh. But Christ had put on that flesh in order to be our Substitute. The Resurrection of that body means, therefore, the continuation of the substitution-ary work of Christ. Yet there is a difference. Christ was our Substitute on earth under the sign of death. There He took our punishment by taking our place under the judgment of God. But now, in His Resurrection, He is under the sign of life. 'Therefore, as He was said to have died for our sins, because, the price of sin having been paid off by His death, He has delivered us from the calamity of death, so now He is said to have been raised for our justification, because He has restored life to us fully by His Resurrection. For first He was struck by the hand of God, that, in the person of a sinner, He might sustain the misery of sin. Then He was exalted into the kingdom of life, that He might give to us His own righteousness and life.'[3] In our surety we receive life. The Resurrection does not lead us away from the substitutionary character of Christ. On the contrary, the element of substitution remains central. Sin was done away with, not that man might be destroyed, but that he might be saved for life with God. The Resurrection is something new, therefore, but yet it is inseparable from the Cross, for it fulfils the purpose of the Cross. 'Wherefore, we divide the cause of our

---

[1] *Comm. in* 1 *Cor.* 15.47, C.R. 77, 599-600.
[2] *Instit.* II.16.13, C.R. 30, 381.
[3] *Comm. in Rom.* 4.25, C.R. 77, 88.

salvation between Christ's death and His Resurrection, because by the former sin was abolished and death was destroyed, and by the latter righteousness was restored and life was established.'[1] As the Cross is the sign that we are dead as sinners, so the Resurrection is the sign that in Him we are alive as righteous men. 'Here arises the lively assurance of our reconciliation with God, because Christ came forth from Hell as the conqueror of death, in order to show that He had the power of a new life at His disposal. Justly, therefore, does Paul say (1 Cor. 15.14) that there will be no Gospel and that the hope of salvation will be empty and fleeting unless we believe that Christ is risen from the dead. For then did Christ obtain righteousness for us and open up our entrance into Heaven; and in short, then our adoption was ratified, when Christ, by rising from the dead, exerted the power of His Spirit and proved Himself to be the Son of God.'[2]

It must be remembered that Calvin does not see the Resurrection apart from the death of Christ even when speaking of the new life that is obtained for us through our Substitute, for the death of Christ is the beginning of the gift of life. 'Christ is called the first-born from the dead and the first fruits of those who rise (1 Cor. 15.20, Col. 1.18), because by His death He began, and by His Resurrection He completed, a new life. Not that when He died the dead were raised immediately, but because His death was the source and commencement of life.'[3] The Resurrection is more than just the revelation of the efficacy of the Cross. It is also the completion of what was begun in that death: our restoration to life. The two form one work for us.[4] The distinction is made between them that we may learn 'that by that sacrifice, by which sins were expiated, our salvation was begun; then by His Resurrection it was completed. For the beginning of righteousness is that we be reconciled to God; the completion, however, is that, death being overcome, life might reign.'[5] Calvin's speaking of Christ's Ascension as the 'completion of the new life'[6] does not contradict this, for the whole work of

---

[1] *Instit.* II.16.13, *C.R.* 30, 380.

[2] *Comm. in Matth.* 28.1, *C.R.* 73, 792. Cf. *Instit.* II.16.13, *C.R.* 30, 380.

[3] *Comm. in Matth.* 27.52, *C.R.* 73, 783.

[4] '*Mortis Christi meminit, imo et sepulturae: ut quemadmodum in his, ita in resurrectione nobis esse similem colligamus. Ergo mortuus est ipse nobiscum, ut nos cum ipso resurgamus.*' *Comm. in 1 Cor.* 15.3, *C.R.* 77, 538.

[5] *Comm. in Rom.* 4.25, *C.R.* 77, 87.   [6] *Comm. in Luc.* 24.31, *C.R.* 73, 809.

Christ as our Substitute is one: His death in our place, His Resurrection for us, and His life with God as the new life of those for whom He died and rose.

2. RAISED AND ASCENDED IN OUR PLACE

As Christ did not die for Himself, so He rose again, not 'in a private capacity, but in order to breathe the odour of life on all believers'.[1] More specifically, Christ rose in a *representative* capacity. 'Therefore, just as Adam did not die for himself alone, but for us all, it follows that Christ in like manner, who is the prototype, did not rise for Himself alone, for He came to restore everything that had been ruined in Adam.'[2] This representative character of Christ's Resurrection is ensured by the fact that He rose in the flesh—in the same body He had taken in order to be our Substitute in death. Calvin can say, therefore, that 'sin was conquered and abolished in our own nature. Accordingly, it certainly follows that our nature truly shares in His victory.'[3] On the basis of our common nature, Christ's Resurrection is a 'down-payment' (*arrha*) on our own resurrection, ensuring that we will rise also.[4] It is not just an example but the first step of our resurrection, for He rose as our Substitute. In him we are already partakers of a new life, accepted by God as righteous in our Substitute.[5] 'And certainly, although with respect to ourselves our salvation is still the object of hope and as yet hidden, nevertheless in Christ we already possess a blessed immortality and glory. . . . It does not yet appear in the members, but only in the head, yet because of the secret union, it belongs truly to the members.'[6] Christians have this new life in eschatological

---

[1] *Comm. in Matth.* 27.52, *C.R.* 73, 783. Cf. *in Heb.* 13.20: 'Christ was raised from death for this end, that *we* might be renewed unto eternal life by the *same* power of God.' *C.R.* 83, 197.

[2] *Comm. in 1 Cor.* 15.21, *C.R.* 77, 545.   [3] *Comm. in Rom.* 8.3, *C.R.* 77, 140.

[4] *Instit.* II.16.13, *C.R.* 30, 381. Cf. III.25.3: 'Christ neither fell under the power of death nor triumphed over it in His Resurrection *sibi privatim, sed inchoatum fuisse in capite quod impleri in omnibus membris necesse est, secundum cuiusque gradum et ordinem.*' *C.R.* 30, 731. In Aquinas, the substitutionary element is lacking here. He sees the Resurrection of Christ as the cause of our resurrection, but he finds the reason for this in Aristotle: '*Illud quod est primum in quolibet genere, est causa omnium eorum quae sunt post.*' *S.T.* III, qu. 56, art. 1.

[5] *Instit.* II.16.13; We learn from Col. 3.1-2, Calvin says, that the Resurrection is not given to us just as an example, '*sed eius fieri virtute docemur ut regeneremur in iustitiam*'. *C.R.* 30, 381.

[6] *Comm. in Eph.* 2.6, *C.R.* 79, 164.

expectation. 'His Resurrection would be in vain, unless He appeared again as their Redeemer and extended to the whole body of the Church the fruit and effect of that power which He revealed in Himself.'[1]

The place of substitution in Calvin's Christology is now clearer. By standing in our place, Christ has not simply endured our punishment for us, so that we might be set free to go our own way, but He has set us in an indissolvable relation to Himself, so that we are bound to Him. By the very closeness of this union, comparable to the union between a body and its head, the death of a part is the death of the whole. Only the head need die for the whole body to die. And if the head then be given life on behalf of the body, that body is already on the way to life, although the full realization of this life may be delayed. But all this is true only so long as the body is in union with the head. Thus we are never to regard ourselves apart from Christ, even as God never regards us apart from Him.

There remains one last step to our final salvation: our new life with God in His Kingdom, and 'by His Ascension, the Lord has opened the way to the Kingdom of Heaven, which had been closed by Adam'.[2] The basis of the claim that Christ opens Heaven to us is the fact that Christ ascended in the same body in which He suffered for us on earth.[3] The unity, therefore, which He has made between Himself and ourselves continues. 'Christ, therefore, who is in Heaven, has clothed Himself with our flesh, that by stretching out a brotherly hand to us He may raise us to Heaven along with Himself.'[4]

But this Ascension was not only *for* us. It was, in all the reality of Christ's substitutionary character, *our own* ascension. 'For since He entered there in our flesh and, as it were, in our name, it follows, as the apostle says, that in a certain manner we sit together with Him now in Heaven (Eph. 2.5), since we do not hope for Heaven with a bare hope, but possess it in our head.'[5]

---

[1] *Comm. in 1 Thess.* 1.10, C.R. 80, 145.

[2] *Instit.* II.16.16, C.R. 30, 382.

[3] *Comm. in Heb.* 9.11, C.R. 83, 110; *Instit.* II.16.14, C.R. 30, 382; IV.17.27, C.R. 30, 1026; *in Phil.* 2.10, C.R. 80, 29.

[4] *Comm. in Joh.* 3.13, C.R. 75, 62.

[5] '*Utpote qui caelum non spe nuda expectemus, sed in capite nostro possideamus.*' *Instit.* II.16.16, C.R. 30, 383. For Aquinas, the session at the Father's right hand is an honour reserved to Christ alone, in which we have no part. It

By the right of substitution, we have our inheritance already. We have it by hope, but hope is no small thing for Calvin.[1] He who would throw this hope into question, he says, 'nearly drags Christ down out of the possession of Heaven', for He entered there in our name.[2]

A further indication that Calvin understands the Ascension of Christ with direct reference to us is the fact that he sees the Ascension as the glorification of God. 'If ever there was a time when God ascended magnificently after He had appeared to have been ingloriously despised, it was when Christ was raised from our low condition and received into the heavenly glory.'[3] But this very glorification of God in the person of the Son teaches us that this glory is for us, 'for, I ask, what need of a new exaltation had He who was the equal of the Father?'[4] We must conclude, therefore, that this glorification, like everything else that Christ received, was meant for us. 'Whatever He affirms concerning Himself ought to be understood as belonging to us. . . . (Isaiah) might have said in one word that Christ will be exalted and will be treated honourably; but by giving Him the title of Servant, he signifies that He will be exalted for our sake.'[5]

On the basis of substitution, we not only have an entrance into Heaven; we possess it already. 'From the connection that we have with Christ, (Paul) proves that our *politiam* is in Heaven, for it is not right that the members should be separated from their Head.'[6] It is true that we continue to live what appears to be a life apart from Christ, but this 'bodily life does not hinder the heavenly life which we possess by faith. "He has made us to sit together in the heavens" (Eph. 1.20). Again, "You are fellow citizens with the saints of the household of God" (Eph. 2.19). And again, "Our conversation is in heaven" (Phil. 3.20). Paul's writings are full of similar testimonies, by which he asserts that while we live in the world, nevertheless we also live in

---

pertains to us only in the sense that 'because Christ is our head, that which was conferred upon Christ was also conferred upon us in Him', as the honour paid to part of a body also honours, in a certain sense, all the body. *S.T.* III, qu. 58, art. 3, 4.   [1] *Instit.* III.2.42, C.R. 30, 432.

[2] *Comm. in Rom.* 10.6: '*Christi enim in coelum adscensio fidem nostram de aeterna vita sic firmare debet, ut Christum poena ipsum e coelorum possessione detrahat, qui dubitat an coeli haereditas parata sit fidelibus, quorum nomine et cause illuc ingressus est.*' C.R. 77, 200.

[3] *Comm. in Eph.* 4.9, C.R. 79, 194.   [4] *Comm. in Phil.* 2.9, C.R. 80, 28.

[5] *Comm. in Isa.* 52.13, C.R. 65, 252.   [6] *Comm. in Phil.* 3.20, C.R. 80, 56.

Heaven, not only because our Head is there, but because, by the right of union, we have a life in common with Him, as it is said in John 14.1f.'[1] Christ remains our Substitute in life as He was in death, for He made a permanent union between Himself and ourselves.

3. CHRIST AS INTERCESSOR

One element of Calvin's doctrine of the Atonement still calls for our attention: Christ's present intercession for us before the Father. Calvin calls this broadly the work of Christ as Mediator,[2] but he refers to it more precisely as the work of Christ as our Advocate. 'Christ was indeed our Advocate then, when He was on earth, but it was a further concession to our weakness that He ascended into Heaven to undertake the office of Advocate. So whenever mention is made of his Ascension into Heaven, this benefit ought to come to mind: that He appears there before God to defend us by His advocacy.'[3] This is also the work of Christ as priest: 'It belongs to a priest to intercede for the people, that they may obtain favour with God. This is what Christ is ever doing, for it was for this purpose that He rose again from the dead.'[4] But whatever the context, the work is the same: 'He is the eternal intercessor, by whose intervention we obtain favour.'[5]

This intercession is eternal, for 'Christ was constituted a priest and a high priest, not for a limited time', but He holds this office forever and has no need of any 'vicar to be substituted in His place'.[6] This is the basis of our confidence in the eternal efficacy of the work performed during Christ's few years on earth, for by His intercession that work is forever held up before God on our behalf.[7] This intercession is based on Christ's work on earth, for it is grounded in the fact that He has already made our business

---

[1] *Comm. in Gal.* 2.20, *C.R.* 78, 199.
[2] *Comm. in Heb.* 9.11, *C.R.* 83, 110. 'As He had put on our flesh and suffered in it, He obtained this privilege for Himself, that He should appear before God now as a Mediator for us.'
[3] *Comm. in Heb.* 9.24, *C.R.* 83, 118.
[4] *Comm. in Heb.* 7.25, *C.R.* 83, 94.
[5] *Instit.* II.15.6, *C.R.* 30, 367; II.16.16, *C.R.* 30, 383.
[6] *Instit.* IV.18.2, *C.R.* 30, 1052; II.11.4, *C.R.* 30, 332.
[7] *Comm. in 1 Joh.* 2.1, *C.R.* 83, 309; *in Act.* 13.39, *C.R.* 76, 307; *Instit.* II.16.16, *C.R.* 30, 383. Cf. Aquinas: '*Passio et mors Christi de cetero non sit iteranda, tamen virtus illius hostiae permanet in aeternum. S.T.*' III, qu. 22, art. 5.

His by taking on our flesh and acting as our Substitute.[1] 'There is a necessary connection between the sacrifice of the death of Christ and His continual intercession. These are the two parts of his priesthood. For Christ is called a priest in this sense, that He once made atonement for our sins by His death in order to reconcile us to God; and now, having entered into the sanctuary of Heaven, He appears in the presence of the Father, in order to obtain grace for us, that we may be heard in His name.'[2] The doctrine of the eternal intercession of Christ on our behalf, whereby 'He turns the eyes of (the Father) to His righteousness, so as to avert them from our sins',[3] is really only another way of saying that God chooses to see us for all eternity only as being in Christ, that He looks at us no longer in ourselves but looks at us and sees only the righteousness of Christ, even as He once looked at Christ upon the Cross and saw only our sin. This way of describing what Calvin has said on this subject is suggested not as an improvement on Calvin but as a reminder of the breadth of his thought.

The question must now be asked whether the idea of Christ as intercessor is compatible with the idea of substitution. Such a question is presented to us by a passage in which Christ is assigned an intermediate position between the Father and men: 'Having entered into the heavenly sanctuary, He alone, till the consummation of the ages, presents to God the prayers of His people who remain at a distance in the forecourt.'[4] There appears to be a separation here between Christ and ourselves that seems at first to limit the concept of substitution. But on second consideration, we must remember that this is a pictorial representation which is only an analogy and not a description of reality. If we do not pay attention to this separation we shall not have understood what Calvin means by our connection with Christ on the basis of His substitutionary work. That separation is a sign of the Lordship of Christ. Christ is our Substitute only as our Lord, to whom we belong, and by whose hand we are supported over the abyss of death. The continual intercession of Christ means our continual dependence on Him and on the work that He did in our

---

[1] *Comm. in Heb.* 9.11, C.R. 83, 110.
[2] *Comm. in 1 Tim.* 2.6, C.R. 80, 272.
[3] *Instit.* II.16.16, C.R. 30, 383.
[4] *Instit.* III.20.20, C.R. 30, 646.

place, for apart from Him we are utterly lost. 'Our lips are not sufficiently pure to celebrate the name of God without the intervention of the priesthood of Christ.'[1] By His intercession alone, we have access to the Father. Commenting on the text, 'We have an advocate with the Father', Calvin says: 'Since (John) wishes to show how we return into favour with God, he says that Christ is our Advocate, for He appears before God for this end, that He may exercise towards us the power and efficacy of His sacrifice. That this may be better understood, I shall speak more crudely: the intercession of Christ is a continual application of His death for our salvation. That God then does not impute to us our sins happens because He considers Christ as intercessor.'[2] Christ is also our Lord, in whom 'the Father wishes to be acknowledged and worshipped'.[3] He is our Substitute, but He is our sovereign, on whom our very existence depends. This understanding of the intercession of Christ is made clear by Calvin's rejection of the idea of Christ standing midway between the Father and ourselves, begging for our deliverance.[4] Such a theory fails to do justice to the glory of Christ and also to His sovereign union with us. The priestly function of Christ is not in conflict with the idea of substitution, for 'in reality an entrance into Heaven is made open to us through the favour of Christ, for He has made us a royal priesthood'.[5] We share in His glory; but the glory of which the love of God has made it possible for us to partake is the glory of our *Lord*, who gave Himself for us and by whom we are sustained and given the first fruits of our eternal life of peace with God.

[1] *Instit.* III.20.28, *C.R.* 30, 655.

[2] *Comm. in* 1 *Joh.* 2.1, *C.R.* 83, 308-309.

[3] *Comm. in Joh.* 5.23, *C.R.* 75, 114; Cf. *in Act.* 4.26, *C.R.* 76, 92; *in Phil.* 2.9, *C.R.* 80, 28.

[4] *Comm. in* 1 *Joh.* 2.1, *C.R.* 83, 310. Aquinas understands the office of Mediator more in this sense of being between God and man. Christ as man is the Mediator, '*quia, secundum quod est homo, distat et a Deo in natura, te ab hominibus in dignitate et gratiae et gloriae*'. S.T. III, qu. 26, art. 2.

[5] *Comm. in Heb.* 10.19, *C.R.* 83, 128.

•

PART III

INCORPORATION:
UNION WITH CHRIST

CHAPTER VII

THE MEANS OF INCORPORATION

1. Substitution and Incorporation

IF we were to stop at this point in Calvin's theology, we should
not have made a true presentation of his doctrine of Reconciliation. At the beginning of Book I of the *Institutes* Calvin
has pointed out the inseparable connection between the knowledge of God and the knowledge of man, so that a knowledge of
an abstract God, as opposed to the God who is *pro nobis* and who
judges and redeems us, is ruled out.[1] But in Book III Calvin
does not simply turn to the man who is reconciled to God, in
order to understand him in the light of his Redeemer. Were
that the case, then we should expect Book III of the *Institutes* to
tell us that we are now to examine how the *completed* reconciliation works out in terms of the life of man. What we find, however, is an explanation of what must happen before the work of
Christ can become effective. The opening of Book III makes it
clear that, for Calvin, God's work of reconciliation is not to be
regarded as complete with the event of Easter. As we pass from
Book II to Book III, we move into the final stage of the work of
reconciliation, and Calvin's understanding of the substitutionary
character of Christ becomes clear only when we follow him into
the area now to be considered, into his teaching about the Holy
Spirit, justification, sanctification and the Church.

This is not to say that in Book III one moves away from Christ
and His work of substitution. On the contrary, that is precisely
what Calvin denies. If it is a question of 'how we obtain' the
enjoyment of all that Christ is and has done for us, then the
answer cannot be by some means apart from Christ, nor on the
other hand, by an abstractly conceived Christ who is 'separated'
from us.[2] It would be an abstraction of substitution, even a denial
of it, to conceive of Him apart from us, simply as existing in and

---

[1] *Instit.* I.1.1, 2, *C.R.* 30, 31 *et seq.*   [2] *Instit.* III.1.1, *C.R.* 30, 393.

for Himself. 'As long as Christ is apart from us and we are separated from Him, all that He suffered and performed for the salvation of the human race is useless and unavailing to us.'[1] If we would not reduce Christ and His work to futile abstractions, then we must see Him always in terms of His substitution, as does the author of Hebrews, who 'does not speak of what Christ is in Himself, but shows what He is to us'.[2]

Calvin does not conceive of substitution as a purely objective work. Corresponding to the substitutionary work of God in Christ *extra nobis*, there is a work of God *in nobis*, and a work that, for Calvin, is as necessary to salvation as the first. 'In whatever way we may have been redeemed by Christ, yet till we are introduced into communion with Him by the calling of the Father, we are both heirs of darkness and death, and enemies of God.'[3] And again, Christ's 'death and Resurrection bear no fruit, except in so far as He calls us to a participation in this grace'.[4] The substitutionary work of Christ is in itself the whole matter of reconciliation, but until we are incorporated into Christ, He 'remains of no value to us, because we look at Him as an object of cold speculation without us, and therefore at a great distance from us. . . . This union alone makes it fruitful to us that He has come in the character of a Saviour.'[5]

The work of God in Christ is not in vain, therefore, and does not remain a potential reconciliation, but is effective for salvation through our incorporation into Him. Christ is not content to provide a means of reconciliation only, but takes us up into His work and makes it effective for us.[6] Commenting on Isaiah 53.10, Calvin says: 'God's kindness is commended to us twice in this passage: first, that He spared not his only-begotten Son, but delivered Him up for us, that He might deliver us from death; and second, that He does not suffer His death to be useless and unprofitable, but causes it to yield very abundant fruit; for the death of Christ would be of no avail to us if we did not experience its fruit and efficacy.'[7] When Calvin speaks of a second commendation of God's kindness here, he does not mean that we are now to leave Christ's work and pass on to something new. This

---

[1] *Instit.* III.1.1, *C.R.* 30, 393.   [2] *Comm. in Heb.* 4.15, *C.R.* 83, 54.
[3] *Instit.* III.14.6, *C.R.* 30, 568.   [4] *Comm. in 2 Tim.* 1.9, *C.R.* 80, 352.
[5] *Instit.* III.1.3, *C.R.* 30, 396.   [6] *Comm. in Isa.* 53.11, *C.R.* 65, 264.
[7] *Comm. in Isa.* 53.10, *C.R.* 65, 264.

second commendation of God's goodness is based on the first, so that there is no moving away from Christ. On the contrary, we come nearer to Christ, by an incorporation made possible by His substitution of Himself in our place.

Incorporation means the realization of substitution. It focuses attention even more strongly on our total dependence on our Substitute, so that Calvin can say that 'believers live out of themselves—that is, they live in Christ'.[1] All our being depends wholly on Him. 'We are by nature barren and dry except in so far as we have been grafted into Christ and draw a power which is new and proceeds from Him.'[2] Apart from our Substitute, we have and are nothing, for 'there is no other life than that which is breathed into us by Christ. Thus we begin to live only when we are grafted into Him and enjoy the same life with Him.'[3] This last passage shows how completely incorporation carries out the meaning of substitution: grafted into Christ, we depend solely on His being in our place, for we 'enjoy the same life with Himself'; in Him is the only life we can have, for in Him we have died on the Cross. Although we might call this incorporation the subjective side of reconciliation, yet here as well as on the objective side of Christ's substitutionary work Calvin is speaking of the work of God, not of the work of man. On Romans 6.5 he says: 'The Apostle does not exhort, but rather proclaims the benefit of Christ, for He requires of us nothing that is done by our exertion or industry, but preaches that grafting which is done by the hand of God.'[4]

In considering God's activity as the Holy Spirit, we must remember that for Calvin the Spirit is the Spirit of Jesus Christ our Substitute. Although that substitution requires incorporation into Christ before it can become effective, still we do not leave Christ's work behind. Incorporation is substitution seen from the side of man, where man is not the active agent but the object of God's reconciliation. It will become clear in the course of our presentation just how little place there is in Calvin's theology for a work of the Holy Spirit that is independent of the work of Christ.

2. INCORPORATION BY THE SPIRIT

Our incorporation into Christ is the work of the Holy Spirit,

[1] *Comm. in Gal.* 2.20, *C.R.* 78, 199.   [2] *Comm. in Joh.* 15.1, *C.R.* 75, 338.
[3] *Comm. in Eph.* 2.4, *C.R.* 79, 163.   [4] *Comm. in Rom.* 6.5, *C.R.* 77, 107.

by whose power 'we are introduced to the enjoyment of Christ'.[1]
God is at work here in a special way of His existence: God in
Christ reaching out to man. This way in which He exists is God
the Holy Spirit. 'The peculiar office of Christ was to appease the
wrath of God by atoning for the sins of the world, to redeem men
from death, to procure righteousness and life; the peculiar office
of the Spirit is to make us partakers not only of Christ Himself,
but of all His blessings. It is not wrong, however, to infer a
distinctio personarum from this passage (*i.e.* "He will send you
another comforter"), for the Spirit must differ in some special
way from the Son, so as to be "another".'[2] The Spirit is God in
'the power and efficacy' of His action, distinct but not different
from God as Father and as Son.[3] But as the supreme action of
God is His action in Christ, so the Spirit is God in the power of
His work of reconciliation: 'He is called the Spirit of Christ, not
only because the eternal Word of God is united with the same
Spirit as the Father, but also with respect to (Christ's) character
as Mediator, for if (Christ) had not been provided with this power
(*i.e.* the Spirit), His coming would have been of no value to us.'[4]
As the Spirit of reconciliation, the Holy Spirit is God drawing
man to Himself. If God did not exist in this way too, then He
would not be what He is for us as Father and as Son: without the
'communion of the Spirit . . . there can be no enjoyment of the
paternal favour of God or the beneficence of Christ'.[5] This too
is a way of the eternal being of God, and a way in which He
exists for us and for our salvation: 'We begin with the gratuitous
mercy of the Father; next, Christ comes forward with the sacrifice of His death; and then the Holy Spirit is also added, by whom
He washes and regenerates us and, in short, makes us partakers
of all His benefits. So we see that God cannot be truly known
unless our faith distinctly conceive of three ways of existence in
one Being.'[6]

The whole purpose of the mercy of God as Father and His
influence upon us as Holy Spirit is to bring us to a participation
in Christ.[7] The Spirit, therefore, 'has chosen His residence in
Christ, that those heavenly riches which we so greatly need may

---

[1] *Instit.* III.1.1, *C.R.* 30, 393.   [2] *Comm. in Joh.* 14.16, *C.R.* 75, 329.
[3] *Instit.* I.13.18, *C.R.* 30, 105.   [4] *Instit.* III.1.2, *C.R.* 30, 395.
[5] Ibid. Cf. IV.17.12, *C.R.* 30, 1011.
[6] *Comm. in Matth.* 28.19, *C.R.* 73, 824.   [7] *Instit.* IV.1.3, *C.R.* 30, 748.

flow out upon us from Him'.[1] In a word, the Spirit is Christ reaching out to men to give them all that He has won. Calvin's way of saying this is that 'the Holy Spirit is the cord by which Christ efficaciously binds us to Himself'.[2] Note that Christ is the author of the union: 'Christ, when He enlightens us with faith by the power of His Spirit, at the same time grafts us into His body, that we may become partakers of all His benefits.'[3]

What is the nature of this union? In what sense are we to understand the concept *incorporation?* For Calvin, the answer is: it is a 'spiritual union', because God effects it by the 'power of His Spirit'.[4] When Calvin calls this union 'spiritual', he does not mean that it is a nebulous connection, for he insists that we are really one with Christ by the work of His Spirit. But he rejects the idea that 'Christ's essence is blended with ours'.[5] Such a blending of substance would not constitute a stronger union, nor is it warranted by Scripture. 'We infer that we are one with the Son of God, not because He pours His substance into us, but because, by the power of His Spirit, He shares with us His life and all the blessings which He has received from the Father.'[6] Calvin would not throw the least doubt on our union with Christ, but he insists on this dogmatic distinction: our union with Christ is not corporeal but spiritual, 'because the secret influence of the Spirit is the bond which unites us to Christ'.[7] The issue is not *that* we are united to Christ, but *how* we are united to Him.

The dogmatic necessity for this assertion is based on the true humanity of Christ. But Christ ascended into Heaven in the same body that He had assumed. The Holy Spirit, therefore, who is able to unite things spacially separated,[8] must unite us on earth with the man Jesus Christ in Heaven. 'Being received up into Heaven, He removed His bodily presence from our sight, not in order to cease to be present with the faithful who were still in a state of pilgrimage on earth, but in order to govern both Heaven and earth by a more efficacious strength'—*i.e.* by the Holy Spirit.[9] By means of His Spirit, Christ reaches down from Heaven and unites us to Himself in a real and eternal union. It

[1] *Instit.* II.15.5, *C.R.* 30, 365.   [2] *Instit.* III.1.1, *C.R.* 30, 394.
[3] *Instit.* III.2.35, *C.R.* 30, 427.
[4] *Comm. in Eph.* 5.32, *C.R.* 79, 226-227.
[5] *Instit.* III.11.5, *C.R.* 30, 536.
[6] *Comm. in Joh.* 17.21, *C.R.* 75, 387.   [7] *Instit.* IV.17.33, *C.R.* 30, 1034.
[8] *Instit.* IV.17.10, *C.R.* 30, 1009.   [9] *Instit.* II.16.14, *C.R.* 30, 381.

H

is, however, a union by the power of the Spirit of Christ, not a
blending of substances. Christ remains Lord and we remain
those whose existence depends totally on Him. There is no identity in Calvin's theology between Christ and Christians; the distinction remains in a union that is activated and realized solely
from the side of Christ. The common nature which we have
with Christ, but which was not in itself sufficient to create this
union, is made the basis of union by the action of the Holy Spirit.

3. INCORPORATION THROUGH FAITH

We shall not have a complete picture of incorporation unless
we look not only at the subject of this action—God as Holy Spirit
—but also at its object: man. Calvin does not turn our attention
to man before he has made it clear that the work of the Spirit is
also an act of the free grace of God, in no sense coming from or
dependent on us. And yet, when God in Christ reaches out to
draw man into union with Himself, there is something to be said
on the side of man. Whatever is said, of course, is not said of
man in Himself, but always of man as the object of the action of
God. Within this framework, Calvin turns our attention to the
work of God *in* man in incorporating him into Christ: the gift of
faith. It is not our concern here to present all that Calvin has to
say on this subject, and we shall confine our attention to the place
of faith in incorporation.

The principal work that the Holy Spirit accomplishes, according
to Calvin, is the gift of faith, the opening up of man to receive
Christ and to know what Christ is for him.[1] It is a sheer 'supernatural gift' of God that He reaches down to us to open us up in
this way.[2] Both in its initiation and in its continuation, this work
is the work of God. 'Not only is the Spirit the originator of faith,
but He increases it by degrees, till He leads us by it into the
Heavenly Kingdom.'[3] Thus from beginning to end, 'faith is the
peculiar and entire work of the Holy Spirit'.[4] Where faith is
found, there is God in Christ at work as the Spirit, and therefore
the assurance of union with Christ: 'Those who now aspire to
Him by faith will in no way be disappointed, for the distance of

---

[1] *Instit.* III.1.4, *C.R.* 30, 396. Cf. IV.1.1: 'By the faith of the Gospel,
Christ becomes ours and we become partakers of the salvation procured by
Him.' *C.R.* 30, 745.   [2] *Ibid.*

[3] *Instit.* III.2.33, *C.R.* 30, 426.   [4] *Instit.* IV.14.8, *C.R.* 30, 947.

position does not prevent believers from possessing Him who fills Heaven and earth by the power of His Spirit.'[1] As the Spirit is the agent of union with Christ, so 'faith is the *medium* by which we are spiritually grafted into the body of Christ'.[2]

Calvin's full definition of faith is: 'a firm and certain knowledge of the divine benevolence towards us, which, being founded on the truth of the gratuitous promise in Christ, is both revealed to our minds and confirmed in our hearts by the Holy Spirit'.[3] It is a knowledge that penetrates the whole man, mind and heart, a knowledge of, and trust in, God's love in Jesus Christ, which comes to us by the power of the Holy Spirit. 'If anyone should wish it to be more clearly expressed, faith consists of a knowledge of Christ.'[4] The nature of faith is essentially knowledge, in the full sense of the word (*i.e.* from the 'heart' as well as from the mind), and its object is Christ. 'This is the proper look of faith: to be fixed on (Christ), in whom it beholds the breast of God filled with love. This is a firm and enduring support, to rely on the death of Christ as the only pledge (of that love).'[5] Faith, then, is a sure reliance on God as He is for us in Christ, and on Christ as our true Substitute before the Father.[6]

Neither God apart from Christ, nor a Christ who is other than God in His work of reconciliation, can be the object of faith. It is true that we are to believe in God, but in God as He is in Christ and not in any other way. 'The secret love with which the Heavenly Father embraced us to Himself is higher than all other causes (of salvation), because it originates in His eternal purpose, but that grace which He wishes to be made known to us and by which we are stirred up to the hope of salvation begins with the reconciliation which was procured through Christ.'[7] In His love God removed the barrier of sin by the substitutionary work of Christ, and so, 'as we first heard (John 3.16) that God, because He loved us, gave His Son to die for us, so it is added immediately that it is Christ alone on whom, strictly speaking,

---

[1] *Comm. in Matth.* 28.1, *C.R.* 73, 793.
[2] *Instit.* II.13.2, *C.R.* 30, 350.   [3] *Instit.* III.2.7, *C.R.* 30, 403.
[4] *Instit.* III.2.8, *C.R.* 30, 404. Cf. *Comm. in Isa.* 53.11, *C.R.* 65, 264-265.
[5] *Comm. in Joh.* 3.16, *C.R.* 75, 64.
[6] Note that there is no question of faith in or union with any sort of God apart from Christ. As for union with such a God, 'we shun and dread every access to Him, unless a Mediator come who can deliver us from fear'. *Comm. in 1 Pet.* 1.21, *C.R.* 83, 226.   [7] *Comm. in Joh.* 3.16, *C.R.* 75, 64.

faith ought to look.'[1] We are to believe in God by believing in Christ: 'for since God is incomprehensible, faith could never reach to him unless it turned to Christ'[2]. And again: 'the kindness of God is not known except when it is revealed by the light of faith',[3] the object of which is Christ. Faith, in short, grasps God in Christ, and it does so in the power of God its giver.[4]

For Calvin, therefore, faith is the *conditio sine qua non* of salvation. 'A community of flesh does not alone constitute a fraternal union', for 'the children of God are born, not of flesh and blood, but of the Spirit through faith'.[5] Until we are united to Christ through faith, we have no part in His redeeming work,[6] for 'by the faith of the Gospel Christ becomes ours and we become partakers of the salvation procured by Him'.[7] As Christ died for all men, so faith in Him is offered to all. 'No one who is teachable and becomes obedient to the Gospel of Christ is excluded from this salvation.'[8] And yet, Calvin was faced with the fact that not all men believe in Christ.[9] Having understood faith as necessary to salvation, he is required to say that we may not have hope for all men, but only for those who believe.

This is the point at which Calvin comes to grips with the major tension in the biblical witness, and Calvin's theology seeks to preserve the tension between the universality of the work of Christ and the fact that not all believe in Him. Christ died for all men in obedience to the Father's will; faith is the gift of God, but only some men receive it. 'Nothing in the world will be found worthy of the favour of God, yet He shows himself to be reconciled to the whole world when He calls all men without exception to the faith of Christ, which is nothing else than the entrance into life. Let us remember, on the other hand, that while life is promised universally to all who believe in Christ, still faith is by no means common to all. For Christ is made known and held out to the sight of all, but the elect alone are

---

[1] *Comm. in Joh.* 3.16, *C.R.* 75, 64.   [2] *Comm. in* 1 *Pet.* 1.21, *C.R.* 83, 226.
[3] *Comm. in Tit.* 3.4, *C.R.* 80, 429. Cf. *in Rom.* 5.17, *C.R.* 77, 100.
[4] *Comm. in Col.* 2.12, *C.R.* 80, 106.
[5] *Instit.* II.13.2, *C.R.* 30, 350.   [6] *Instit.* III.1.1, *C.R.* 30, 393.
[7] *Instit.* IV.1.1, *C.R.* 30, 745. 'Neither He nor his blessings become ours, except in so far as we embrace them and Him by faith.' *Comm. in Heb.* 5.9, *C.R.* 83, 64.
[8] *Comm. in Heb.* 5.9, *C.R.* 83, 64. Cf. *in Joh.* 5.25, *C.R.* 75, 118.
[9] 'The Father has offered and presented Christ to all for salvation, but He is not known and received by all.' *Instit.* IV.14.7, *C.R.* 30, 945-946.

those whose eyes God opens, that they may seek Him by faith.'[1]
We are asked to pray that all men may be saved, for we do not
know which men have been chosen to be saved; but we do know
that God will save only those whom he has elected to salvation,
and not the 'reprobate'.[2]

First let us notice what Calvin has not done here. He has not
resolved the tension by retreating to a position of limited atonement. Christ died for all in the place of all and is offered to all.
On that there is no compromise. But Calvin has also refused to
ease the tension by taking up a position of universalism, whereby
all are to be saved. Calvin had too clear a sense of the majesty
and righteousness of God and he was too loyal to the biblical
witness to say that. The next point is to notice from what point
of view Calvin considers the tension. He looks at it under the
aspect of God's eternal election. But he does not do so in a
mechanical doctrine of a simple double predestination. It is true
that Calvin believed that some were predestined to damnation,
but he never gave this the same importance as election to salvation. Reprobation is the reverse side of election, the darkness
that is in contrast to the light. Reprobation is secondary and
derived. Election is primary and direct. This is clear in the
passages just quoted or referred to. It should also be noted that
for Calvin there is a complete suspension of judgment on this
matter. Never does he try to draw a line or even trace out among
men the line he believed God to have drawn between the elect
and the reprobate. All he will do is to set up the two sides, out
of balance as it were, with the emphasis falling on election. He
refuses to seek to know what has not been revealed. He will pray
for all men, but this prayer is eschatologically qualified, for God's
elect will be revealed in the Last Day. This eschatological note
of suspended knowledge and judgment is an integral part of
Calvin's doctrine of predestination, which may, strictly speaking,
be called a doctrine of double predestination, but one in which
the two sides are deliberately unbalanced.

It is not our concern to enter into a close examination of
Calvin's doctrine of predestination in this study. We have sum-
marized here our understanding of Calvin on this matter simply
because it was inescapable. One more point may be made in this
connection. As we have said, Calvin regards the tension between

[1] *Comm. in Joh.* 3.16, C.R. 75, 65.   [2] *Comm. in Joh.* 17.9, C.R. 75, 380.

the universality of Christ's work and the fact that only some men believe under the aspect of God's election. Without resolving the tension in either of the directions mentioned, he might have chosen a different course. Here we would recall all the questions we have raised so far in the course of this study, bearing on the involvement of God in the work of Christ, as Calvin understood it. Had Calvin seen the Son of God Himself as our Substitute, and therefore the substitutionary work of Christ as the unqualified reality of our salvation, he might have understood faith as the knowledge, held only by a few, of what God has done for *all* men in Christ, whether they know it or not. Has not Calvin insisted that faith is essentially knowledge, and also that Christ took the place of all men? Faith could then be a witness to Christians of the truth about Christ, which is the truth about all men because He represents all men, and believers would then be those who confessed their incorporation into Christ by His substitution of Himself in our place, and who had the mission to proclaim this reality, valid in itself for all men, to the world. Then Calvin could have continued to see faith as a gift, as a miracle, and as a prerequisite for membership in the Church, in that community which has the special commission from God to proclaim to the world the good news of the reconciliation accomplished in Christ. Such a position approaches universalism only if we insist on developing it strictly according to logic. But if we insist, as Calvin does, upon the sovereign freedom of God, we are left with reason to hope for all men, even though, again with Calvin, we must maintain an eschatological suspension of knowledge and judgment about the ultimate decision of God in the case of any particular man. Tension remains, but here it is considered under the aspect of God's sovereign freedom. This position is suggested by way of contrast to Calvin's in order to show that the issue raised by his understanding of predestination is not one of tension versus no tension, but one of how the tension is to be regarded, and that Calvin's position here is consistent with his basic understanding of the substitutionary character of Christ.

But although Calvin understands saving faith as a gift of God on the basis of an eternal election, that does not mean that he sees man as a mere pawn of his destiny. 'I do acknowledge that it belongs to God alone to open the eyes of the blind, and that no man is qualified to understand the mysteries of the Heavenly

Kingdom unless God enlighten him inwardly by His Spirit; but it does not follow from this that they who perish through their own brute blindness are excusable.'[1] It must be remembered that not only Christ but also faith in Him is offered to all men. Those who refuse this gift do so by their own act for which they are responsible. Predestination, as Calvin sees it, is an explanation of *why* some refuse and others accept. It finds its place near the end of Book III of the *Institutes*, not at the beginning. The unbeliever is what he is through his own fault: 'The blame lies *solely* with ourselves if we do not become partakers of this salvation, for (God) calls all men to Himself without a single exception and gives Christ to all, that we may be enlightened by Him.'[2] Unbelievers exclude themselves from God's love: 'Were it not that the reprobate, through their own fault, turn life into death, the Gospel would be to all the power of God unto salvation.'[3] In itself, the work of Christ remains for all men, whether it is refused by some or not. Commenting on the text, 'If we are unbelieving, he remains faithful', Calvin says: 'The meaning is that our faithlessness takes nothing from the Son of God or from His glory, because, being complete in Himself, He is in no need of our confession.'[4] This is as close as Calvin comes to the other way of understanding faith that we have just mentioned, but he does not work out consequently the thought that Christ is what He is in Himself, quite apart from our faith in Him.

To believers, however, faith is the sure sign of their union with Christ, for 'Christ, when He illuminates us with faith by the power of His Spirit, at the same time grafts us into His body, that we may become partakers of all His benefits'.[5] By the medium of faith, we are 'united into one body with Him'.[6] Faith cannot be an abstract or speculative knowledge of Christ, for it is an awareness of our dependence on Him and of the union that He has made between Himself and us by becoming our Substitute and drawing us to Himself to share in all that He has accomplished in our place. Faith is the sign of incorporation in the fullest sense of the word. 'I acknowledge that it is only after we obtain Christ

[1] *Comm. in Luc.* 19.42, C.R. 73, 577.   [2] *Comm. in Isa.* 42.6, C.R. 65, 65.
[3] *Comm. in Matth.* 16.19, C.R. 73, 475. Cf. *in Luc.* 12.51, C.R. 73, 292.
[4] *Comm. in 2 Tim.* 2.13, C.R. 80, 365.   [5] *Instit.* III.2.35, C.R. 30, 427.
[6] *Comm. in Matth.* 12.48, C.R. 73, 350. Cf. *in 1 Joh.* 3.5: 'He says that the faithful abide in Christ, because we are grafted into Him by faith and made one with Him.' C.R. 83, 334.

Himself that we become partakers of Christ's benefits. However, He is obtained, I affirm, not alone when we believe that He was made an offering for us, but when He dwells in us, when He is one with us, when we are members of His flesh, when, in short, we are incorporated into Him into one life and substance, as it were.'[1] There is no question of an abstract substitution, 'for faith does not look at Christ as though He were far off, but it embraces Him, that He may become ours and dwell in us. It causes us to be incorporated into His body, to have life in common with him, and, in short, to become one with Him.'[2] For the believing man, reconciliation is complete. 'As we are grafted into the body of Christ by faith, we are adopted by God as His children.'[3] The fullness of our redemption is not yet ours, but we await the full enjoyment of our salvation with a sure hope, knowing that what we enjoy now by faith will certainly be ours in the Kingdom of God. On Titus 3.5, Calvin says: 'He speaks of faith, and teaches that we have already obtained salvation. Although, involved in sin, we carry about a body of death, yet we are certain of our salvation, provided that we are grafted into Christ by faith, according to that saying, "He who believes in the Son of God has passed from death into life" (John 5.24). Yet shortly afterwards, by introducing the word *faith*, he shows that we have not yet actually attained what Christ procured for us by His death. Hence it follows that, on the part of God, our salvation is completed, while the full enjoyment of it is delayed till the end of our warfare. And that is what the same apostle teaches in another passage: that we are saved by hope (Rom. 8.24).'[4] Faith is thus the sign of incorporation under an eschatological aspect, and the medium of that incorporation which we shall fully enjoy only in the Kingdom of God.

[1] *Comm. in* 1 *Cor.* 11.24, C.R. 77, 487.
[2] *Comm. in Joh.* 6.35, C.R. 75, 145.
[3] *Comm. in Matth.* 22.30, C.R. 73, 606.
[4] *Comm. in Tit.* 3.5, C.R. 80, 430. Cf *in Matth.* 22.30, C.R. 73, 606.

CHAPTER VIII

THE CONSEQUENCE OF INCORPORATION

1. JUSTIFICATION AND SANCTIFICATION

W̲E have examined Calvin's understanding of the foundation of reconciliation in Christ's substitution of Himself
in our place, and the realization of reconciliation in our
incorporation into Christ. We are now in a position to consider
what light is thrown on Calvin's understanding of some of the
main Christian doctrines, when seen from the centre of his
theology. Our choice of the subjects to be considered is guided in
part by Calvin himself, in part by our subject; we take the subjects which play the largest part in the remainder of the *Institutes*
and which at the same time bear particularly on what has been
said already. We turn therefore to review Calvin's teaching in
the areas of justification and sanctification in this chapter, and
the Church and Sacraments in the concluding chapter, in the
light of Calvin's understanding of reconciliation as substitution
and incorporation.

On the basis of Christ's substitutionary work, we become one
with Christ, having a real, spiritual union with Him. But since
the Christ is the Righteous and Holy One of God, union with
Christ must mean union with Him in His righteousness and in
His holiness. We find, therefore, that the greater portion of
Book III of the *Institutes* is given over to the examination of these
two major aspects of the Christian faith, for 'the substance of the
Gospel is said not without reason to be contained in repentance
(*poenitentia*) and remission of sins', *i.e.* sanctification and justification.[1] The method of Calvin's exposition of these doctrines
has been the cause of discussion, for he takes up the doctrine of
sanctification before turning to that of justification.[2] Having

---

[1] *Instit.* III.3.1, *C.R.* 30, 434.
[2] Cf. J. Wendel, *Calvin, sources et évolution de sa pensée religieuse.* Presses
Univ. de France, Paris, 1950, p. 175.

spoken first of the Holy Spirit, and then of the gift of faith,
Calvin explains the order he intends to follow in these words:
'Since Christ confers both on us, and we obtain both by faith,
that is, newness of life and gratuitous reconciliation, the regular
method of instruction requires me to enter here on the discussion
of both. But our transition will be from faith to repentance,
because, when this point is well understood, it will better appear
how man is justified by faith alone and by sheer pardon, and yet
that real sanctity of life, so to speak, is not separated from the
gratuitous imputation of righteousness.'[1] The order followed is
not that of importance, for both should, if it were possible, be
treated together to show that they are two inseparable aspects of
the Gospel. But Calvin says that he will begin with sanctification
in order to help our understanding of both and also their inseparable connection. Since sanctification is only partial, as we
shall see, Calvin may have treated it first to make sure that the
reader would not consider it of lesser importance: 'Christ is made
unto us righteousness and sanctification (1 Cor. 1.30). The former
we obtain by a gratuitous acceptance, and the latter by the gift
of the Holy Spirit when we are made new men. There is, however, an inseparable connection between these two favours. Let
us, however, take notice that this holiness is only begun in us
and makes progress every day, but it will not be perfected until
Christ appears for the restoration of all things.'[2]

It is above all the indissoluble connection between these two
aspects of the Gospel that Calvin emphasizes. Since both have
their origin in faith, they cannot be separated in time, as though
we believed first and later received sanctification.[3] There is,
moreover, an inner connection between them: 'We cannot be
justified freely through faith alone without at the same time
living holily. For these free gifts are connected, as if by an indissoluble bond, so that he who attempts to sever them does in a
manner tear Christ in pieces.'[4] We are, therefore, to avoid all
attempts to consider one as being independent of the other, for to
separate them is to tear Christ apart. Calvin can say this because
he sees both justification and sanctification in Christ Himself, in
our Substitute. We receive His righteousness and holiness because we are united to Him by His Spirit. 'Christ is not truly

---

[1] *Instit.* III.3.1, *C.R.* 30, 434.   [2] *Comm. in Col.* 1.22, *C.R.* 80, 91.
[3] *Instit.* III.3.2, *C.R.* 30, 435.   [4] *Comm. in 1 Cor.* 1.30, *C.R.* 77, 331.

acknowledged as a Saviour until, on the one hand, we learn to receive a free pardon of our sins and know that we are accounted righteous before God because we are freed from guilt, and until, on the other hand, we ask from Him the Spirit of righteousness and holiness, abandoning confidence in all our works and power.'[1]

Calvin also insists that there be no confusion between justification and sanctification. 'These two offices of Christ are joined in such a manner as to be nevertheless distinguished from each other. What Paul here (1 Cor. 1.30) expressly distinguishes, therefore, must not be mistakenly confused.'[2] To make his position clear, we shall quote his explanation of the matter at length: 'The grace of justification is inseparable from regeneration, although they are distinct things. But since it is sufficiently known from experience that some relics of sin always remain in the righteous, the manner of their justification must necessarily be very different from that of their regeneration to newness of life. For God commences the latter in His elect and carries it on gradually and sometimes slowly, throughout the whole course of their lives, so that (seen in themselves) they are always liable to the sentence of death at His tribunal. He justifies them, however, not in a partial manner, but so completely that they may appear in Heaven as if clothed in the purity of Christ.'[3] Because of this difference, we shall also treat the two subjects separately.

We must first, however, call attention to the unity of justification and sanctification upon which Calvin insists so strongly. Both are the work of the Holy Spirit, apprehended by faith, and there can be no separation of the two.[4] This unity is of particular relevance to our subject, because Calvin sees both justification and sanctification as the consequences of our incorporation into Christ. Because Christ stands before the Father in our place, we are accounted righteous by God.[5] Our holiness is also a consequence of our being in Christ, for 'it is He alone in whom we are adopted, and therefore, it is He alone through whom we are made partakers of the Spirit, who is the earnest and witness of our adoption. Paul therefore teaches us by this word (Titus 3.6, "through Jesus Christ") that the Spirit of regeneration is bestowed

---

[1] *Comm. in Matth.* 1.21, C.R. 73, 65.
[2] *Comm. in 1 Cor.* 1.30, C.R. 77, 331. Cf. *in Joh.* 3.16, C.R. 75, 65.
[3] *Instit.* III.11.11, C.R. 30, 542.   [4] *Comm. in 1 Pet.* 1.2, C.R. 83, 209.
[5] *Comm. in Rom.* 5.18, C.R. 77, 101.

on none but those who are members of Christ.'[1] Not in an order of time, but in an order of cause, sanctification is a consequence of incorporation. Only those who are in Christ are sanctified, for the Spirit of Holiness is the Spirit of Jesus Christ, God in Christ reaching out to draw men up into union with their Lord. He who thinks that free pardon is an excuse for irresponsible action has yet to understand the meaning of being in Christ. Calvin takes up sanctification first, in order to avoid just this error, although the two ideas are essentially one.[2] Commenting on the text, 'Yet not I, but Christ lives in me', Calvin says: 'This explains what (Paul) meant by "living unto God". He no longer lives by his own life, but is animated by the secret power of Christ, so that Christ may be said to live and grow in him; for as the soul enlivens the body, so Christ imparts life to His members. It is a remarkable sentiment, that believers live outside of themselves—that is, they live in Christ—which can only be accomplished by holding real and actual communication with Him. Christ lives in us in two ways. The one life consists in His governing us by His Spirit and directing all our actions; the other in His making us partakers of His righteousness, so that while we can do nothing of ourselves, we are accepted in the sight of God in Him. The first pertains to regeneration, the second to justification by free grace.'[3] Free pardon and holiness of life are two functions of our life in Christ no more separable than the being of Christ Himself.

2. SANCTIFICATION BY INCORPORATION

The life of holiness is designated by Calvin by the word *poenitentia*, repentance, which he defines as 'a true conversion of our life to God, proceeding from a sincere and serious fear of God, and consisting in the mortification of our flesh and of the old man, and in a vivification of the Spirit'.[4] It means 'a transformation, not only in external actions, but in the soul itself',[5] and is motivated by fear, arising from 'a knowledge of the divine judgment'.[6] It consists of a dying and rising that reveals that sanctification is the consequence of incorporation into our Substitute: 'Both (parts of repentance) result from our participation in Christ. For if we truly share in His death, our old man is crucified by its

---

[1] *Comm. in Tit.* 3.6, *C.R.* 80, 431-432.
[3] *Comm. in Gal.* 2.20, *C.R.* 78, 199.
[5] *Instit.* III.3.6, *C.R.* 30, 438.
[2] *Instit.* III.3.1, *C.R.* 30, 434.
[4] *Instit.* III.3.5, *C.R.* 30, 437.
[6] *Instit.* III.3.7, *C.R.* 30, 438.

power and the body of sin expires, so that the corruption of our former nature loses all its force (Rom. 6.6). If we are partakers of His Resurrection, we are raised by it to a newness of life which corresponds to the righteousness of God.'[1] The foundation of this teaching is the substitutionary work of Christ. If Christ was truly in our place, if He died and rose not for Himself but in our name, and if He then draws us to Himself by His Spirit, so that we become one with Him by faith, then the consequence can only be that we become slowly conformed to Him, His death and Resurrection engraving their mark on the whole of our being and activity. 'This restoration is not accomplished in a single moment or day or year, but by continual and sometimes even slow advances God destroys the corruption of the flesh in His elect, purifies them from all pollution, and consecrates them as temples to Himself, renewing all their senses to real purity, that they may employ their whole lives in the exercise of repentance, and know that this warfare will be ended only by death.'[2]

Sanctification places an imperative upon the Christian: he is called to conform his life to that of Christ. But this imperative is based on the indicative: the event of God's mercy in Jesus Christ. This is to be seen already in the preaching of Jesus, in His proclamation that the Kingdom of God is at hand, upon which He calls for repentance (Mark 1.15). '*First* he declares that the treasures of the mercy of God are opened in Himself, *then* He requires repentance.'[3] If Christ is our pattern, it is only because He is first of all our Saviour.[4] Because Christ has made Himself our Substitute, He has a claim upon us and all our activity. 'If we are not our own, but the Lord's, it is clear both from what errors we must flee and to what end all the actions of our life are to be directed. We are not our own; therefore neither *our* reason nor will should predominate in our thoughts and actions. We are not our own; therefore let us not make it our aim to seek what may be expedient for us according to the flesh. We are not our own; therefore let us forget ourselves and everything we have as far as possible. On the contrary, we are God's; for Him, therefore, let us live and die. We are God's; therefore let *His* wisdom and will rule all our actions. We are God's; therefore let every part of

---

[1] *Instit.* III.3.9, *C.R.* 30, 440.   [2] Ibid.
[3] *Instit.* III.3.19, *C.R.* 30, 449.
[4] *Instit.* III.6.3, *C.R.* 30, 503.

our lives be directed towards Him as our only legitimate end
(Rom. 14.8).'[1]

If this is Calvin's position, why does he speak of the fear of
God's judgment as the basis of sanctification? 'Before the mind
of a sinner can be inclined to repentance,' he says, 'it must be
excited by a knowledge of the divine judgment.'[2] Would it not
have been more consistent with the wonderful passage just quoted
if he had said that a sinner can be turned to repentance only when
excited by a knowledge of the *love* of God revealed in Jesus Christ?
Calvin has said that repentance has its origin in faith, without
which it cannot exist.[3] He lays great stress on the fact that faith
has Christ and the grace of God revealed in Him as its object, not
the wrath and judgment of God.[4] How then can the fear of God
be an incentive for holiness? Surely the inconceivable love shown
in God's forgiveness would be a more compelling basis for sanctification. In fact, precisely on the grounds of all that Calvin has
said about faith and the love of God, God's mercy and love can
be the *only* motivation for sanctification. Would this idea not
have been the only consequential development of his point that
the imperative of the Gospel is based solely on its indicative?

When Calvin speaks of the holiness of Christians, he means
primarily the holiness of Christ, in whom every Christian has
his being, and only secondarily the holiness that they actually
achieve. Christ is the standard of the holiness of believers, and
they are called holy 'because they aspire with all their effort
towards holiness and perfect purity', and then 'the goodness of
God attributes to them that sanctity to which they have not yet
fully attained'.[5] Our holiness is that of our Substitute. 'For as,
in order to obliterate the guilt of the disobedience which had
been perpetrated in our flesh, He assumed to Himself that very
flesh, that He might perform a perfect obedience in it on our
account and in our stead, so he was conceived by the Holy Spirit,
that, having the whole body which He assumed fully endued
with the sanctity of the Spirit, He might communicate the same
to us.'[6] There are two aspects of holiness here. First, we are
holy because Christ is holy. This is the primary aspect of sanctification and it rests solely on substitution. But Calvin says that a

---

[1] *Instit.* III.7.1, *C.R.* 30, 505-506.   [2] *Instit.* III.3.7, *C.R.* 30, 438.
[3] *Instit.* III.3.5, *C.R.* 30, 437.   [4] *Instit.* III.2.7, *C.R.* 30, 402.
[5] *Instit.* IV.1.17, *C.R.* 30, 760.   [6] *Instit.* IV.16.18, *C.R.* 30, 989.

second aspect takes place in us. There is, therefore, a two-sidedness here, as there is in substitution and in incorporation. We are holy by the holiness of Christ in our place, but there is also a result of this' within our lives, for 'in His own person (Christ) has presented us to the Father in a certain manner, *in order that* we may be renewed to true holiness by His Spirit'.[1]

Because sanctification is based on Christ as our Substitute, the life of holiness means a conformity to the life of Christ, and the outstanding characteristic of Christ is His death and Resurrection. Sanctification must entail, therefore, the conformation of our lives to the death and Resurrection of Christ. As there was first Good Friday and then Easter, so there is an order in the dying and rising of the believer. 'No one can rise again with Christ if he has not first died with Him. Hence (Paul) draws an argument from rising again to dying, as from a consequent to an antecedent, showing that we must be dead to the world that we may live to Christ. Why has he taught that we must seek those things that are above? It is because the life of the godly is above. Why does he now teach that the things which are on earth are to be left off? Because (the godly) are dead to the world: "Death precedes that resurrection of which I have spoken; hence both of them must be seen in you." '[2] If Christ remains truly our Substitute, and if we are to be conformed to Him, we must be conformed to Him in his death and sufferings.

That is not to say that Christ is simply our pattern, and that we are asked to follow His example on our own: 'Let us note that the apostle does not simply exhort us here (Rom. 6.4) to an imitation of Christ, as if he said that the death of Christ is to be taken for an example which all Christians are to follow. Surely he goes higher; for he delivers a teaching from which he later draws exhortation, as is apparent. And this is the teaching: that the death of Christ is effectual to extinguish and banish the depravity of the flesh, and His Resurrection is effectual to raise up the newness of a better nature.'[3] A simple idea of the imitation of Christ would miss the whole significance of His substitutionary character and of our incorporation into Him by the power of His

---

[1] *Comm. in Joh.* 17.19, C.R. 75, 385.
[2] *Comm. in Col.* 3.3, C.R. 80, 118. Cf. *in 2 Tim.* 2.11, C.R. 80, 364-365.
[3] *Comm. in Rom.* 6.4, C.R. 77, 105.

Spirit. Our dying is not something we do of ourselves, but a dying with Christ, in the power and efficacy of His death in our place. 'We ought, therefore, to hold fast to this fellowship: that we do not die apart, but along with Christ, in order that we may afterwards have a life in common with Him; that we suffer with Him in order that we may share in His glory.'[1]

Consequently, the first half of sanctification is our mortification. 'Let everyone, therefore, who has become through faith a partaker of all Christ's benefits, acknowledge that a condition is presented to him: that his whole life be conformed to His death.'[2] The whole of what, after the flesh, we call our lives, can be in fact only death. All suffering and persecution are nothing other than the working out in our lives of the reality of the substitutionary character of our Lord,[3] and they are a cause for joy rather than sorrow.[4] Yet mortification does not mean that we should die like Christ by a natural death, but that we have this congruency with His death, that as He died in the flesh which He received of us, so we should die in ourselves that we may live in Him.'[5] Substitution, therefore, entails our conformity to our Substitute. The meaning of Romans 8.29, Calvin says, is that 'God has so decreed, that whoever He has adopted, the same should bear the image of Christ; for He did not simply say, that they might be conformed to Christ, but to the *image of Christ*, in order to show that there is a lively and clear example in Christ which is set before all the sons of God to imitate.'[6] Calvin can speak of an imitation of Christ in this sense, an imitation that is derived from the substitutionary character of Christ's humility. 'He, who was so far above us, willingly came down to our condition, in order that He might enliven us by His own example.'[7] On the other hand, Calvin points out that one may speak of an imitation of Christ only in the loosest sense, for our imitation is extremely inexact. 'Christ's humility consisted in His abasing

[1] *Comm. in 2 Tim.* 2.11, C.R. 80, 365. Cf. *in Matth.* 10.38: 'Let us bear in mind this consolation, that in bearing the Cross, we are the companions of Christ.' *C.R.* 73, 294.

[2] *Comm. in Phil.* 3.10, C.R. 80, 50.

[3] 'They have been called to the faith of Christ on this condition: that they endure persecutions on His account; as though (Paul) had said that their adoption can no more be separated from the Cross, than Christ can be torn asunder from Himself.' *Comm. in Phil.* 1.29, C.R. 80, 27.

[4] *Comm. in Phil.* 2.9, C.R. 80, 27.   [5] *Comm. in Rom.* 6.5, C.R. 77, 107.

[6] *Comm. in Rom.* 8.29, C.R. 77, 160.   [7] *Comm. in Heb.* 12.3, C.R. 83, 173.

Himself from the highest pinnacle of glory to the lowest ignominy; our humility consists in refraining from exalting ourselves
by a false estimation. He gave up His right; all that is required
of us is that we do not assume to ourselves more than is our
due. . . . Since, then, the Son of God descended from so great a
height, how unreasonable that we, who are nothing, should be
lifted up with pride!'[1]

Our mortification is not so much a matter of our following the
example of Christ as it is a work of God in us, whereby He makes
effective in our lives the chief fact of our existence—namely, that
we were in reality put to death in Christ upon the Cross of
Calvary. 'The Scripture sometimes mentions both: that is, that
the Lord tries us with troubles and adversities, that we might be
conformed to the death of Christ; and also that the old man has
been crucified in the death of Christ, that we might walk in
newness of life.'[2] There is no question as to which of these is
primary for Calvin. Our death in Christ is the foundation of our
present mortification: '(Paul) says that this old man is fastened to
the Cross of Christ, because through its power he is slain. And
he alludes precisely to the Cross, that he might show expressly
how we have mortification in no other way than by participation
in His death.'[3] This is accomplished by His Spirit which grafts
us 'into His death, in order that it may be effectual in crucifying
our flesh'.[4] Mortification is the consequence and therefore the
sign of incorporation, so that we may understand our suffering
as a witness of our existence in our crucified Lord. 'To you, (Paul)
says, it is given not only to believe in Christ but also to suffer for
Him. Therefore, even the sufferings themselves are witnesses to
you of the grace of God; and since this is so, you have from this
source a token of salvation.'[5] As long as we continue in this
world, we continue under the sign of the Cross, in which we
have our salvation. We have it now in a state of warfare, a dying
daily to sin, but we have it in a sure hope that Christ's work will

[1] *Comm. in Phil.* 2.6, *C.R.* 80, 25.
[2] *Comm. in* 1 *Pet.* 2.24, *C.R.* 83, 252.
[3] *Comm. in Rom.* 6.6, *C.R.* 77, 107.
[4] *Comm. in* 1 *Pet.* 4.1, *C.R.* 83, 270.
[5] *Comm. in Phil.* 1.28, *C.R.* 80, 21. Cf. *in Col.* 1.24: 'As Christ suffered once
in His own person, so He suffers daily in His members, and in this way there are
filled up the sufferings which the Father has appointed for His body by His
decree. . . . The fellowship that we have with Him extends to this also.'
C.R. 80, 93.

I

be completed in us in the Kingdom of God.[1] Mortification is the character of the life of believers in this time between the victory of Christ and its full revelation.[2]

The whole purpose of the death of Christ, and therefore of our mortification, however, is that we might live a new life, reconciled to God.[3] United to Christ by His Spirit through faith, we are united to Him in His Resurrection as we have been united to Him in His death. He is and remains our Substitute. Therefore, He lives in glory in our place and for us. Death itself cannot take this from us. 'As a graft has the condition of life and death in common with the tree into which it is grafted, so it is reasonable that we should be partakers of the life no less than the death of Christ. For if we are grafted into the likeness of the death of Christ, and that is not without His Resurrection, then no more shall our death be without a resurrection.'[4] This second part of sanctification, our new life in Christ, is not, however, to be regarded as only future, as simply a resurrection in the Day of the Lord. The new life in Christ is ours already, so that 'there is no impropriety in saying that we have *already* passed from death to life; for the incorruptible seed of life resides in the children of God, . . . and they already sit by hope in the heavenly glory with Christ'.[5] If we think that Christ's risen life is only a proof that we also shall have a resurrection, then we have failed to realize the point that Calvin stresses about the Easter event. The Resurrection of Christ was a resurrection in our place, Christ being raised as our Substitute, so that in Him we have already a new life, beginning with Easter morning. 'We only know aright our Lord's Resurrection, if by taking confidence, we dare to rejoice that *we have been made partakers of the same life.*'[6] Also in this part of Calvin's doctrine of sanctification, the foundation is our incorporation into our Substitute.

The new life that we have is that of Christ. But, as Christ has ascended to the Father, our life is hid with Him from human

---

[1] 'He once appeared with a sacrifice to abolish sins; at His second coming He will reveal openly the efficacy of His death, so that sin will have no more power to hurt us.' *Comm. in Heb.* 9.28, *C.R.* 83, 120.

[2] *Comm. in Phil.* 2.10, *C.R.* 80, 29.

[3] *Comm. in 1 Pet.* 3.18, *C.R.* 83, 264.

[4] *Comm. in Rom.* 6.5, *C.R.* 77, 106. Cf. *in 1 Thess.* 4.14, *C.R.* 80, 165.

[5] *Comm. in Joh.* 5.24, *C.R.* 75, 116.

[6] *Comm. in Matth.* 28.10, *C.R.* 73, 799. Cf. *in Gal.* 2.20, *C.R.* 78, 199.

sight. 'It is worthy of observation that our life is said to be hid, that we may not murmur or complain if our earthly life, being buried under the ignominy of the Cross and under various distresses, differs in nothing from death, but that we may patiently wait for the day of revelation. And in order that our waiting may not be painful, let us note those expressions, *in God*, and *with Christ*, which tell us that our life is out of danger, although it is not visible.'[1] The true centre of our existence, therefore, must be there where our Substitute lives for us. 'Ascension follows resurrection; thus, if we are members of Christ, we must ascend into Heaven, because He, on being raised from the dead, was received up into Heaven, that He might draw us up with Him.'[2]

A reflection of this new, invisible life of a believer, is found, however, in this world. Not that sanctification 'consists in a visible parade of ceremonies, but it is a firm faith, a pure conscience, and a cleanness of soul and body which originate in and are completed by the Spirit of God'.[3] In the sight of God, believers are reformed by the Spirit of Holiness, and this change is partially mirrored in their lives. Speaking of the first Christians, Calvin says: 'They were changed for the better and became new men, in consequence of God having mercy on them; as if (the apostle) had said, "When God regenerated you by his Spirit, then did you begin to differ from others." '[4] The Christian can hardly boast of this change, however, for he accomplishes but little. This is the reason for the tension in the Christian life, described in Romans 7.7ff, a conflict whose intensity is unknown to unbelievers, who do not know the meaning of the constant failure to do God's will.[5] The change in our lives by reflection from our sanctification is only begun here, and 'the remnant of the flesh which remains always follows its corrupt affections, and so makes war against the Spirit'.[6] The life of holiness, therefore, is a life of combat, but because we are one with 'the Author of Holiness', our holiness may not be called into question by our failures,[7] for we know that our conformation to our Lord, which is only begun here, will finally be perfected: 'The final end of our adoption is

---

[1] *Comm. in Col.* 3.3, *C.R.* 80, 118.   [2] *Comm. in Col.* 3.1, *C.R.* 80, 117.
[3] *Comm. in Heb.* 10.22, *C.R.* 83, 130.
[4] *Comm. in Tit.* 3.4, *C.R.* 80, 428. Cf. *in Isa.* 42.4: 'Christ's ministry will not be unfruitful, but will have such efficacy that men shall be reformed by it.' *C.R.* 65, 62.   [5] *Comm. in Rom.* 7.15, *C.R.* 77, 129-130.
[6] *Comm. in Rom.* 7.15, *C.R.* 77, 130.   [7] *Comm. in Heb.* 2.11, *C.R.* 83, 28.

that what has in order preceded in Christ shall finally be completed in us.'[1] Sanctification, having its foundation in our incorporation into our Substitute, is the working out under an
→ eschatological aspect of our union with Christ.

3. Justification by Incorporation

Having established that the Christian is called to live a new
life on the basis of his incorporation into Christ, Calvin turns our
attention to the other benefit of our existence in our Substitute:
our justification.[2] We are not only made righteous and holy, we
not only strive continually to conform our lives to that of Christ
and to obtain that perfect righteousness which will be ours in
the Kingdom of God. We are also accepted by God as completely
righteous, not on the basis of what we shall be, but on the basis
of what we are already in Christ. That is the meaning of justification. It is 'an acceptance, by which God receives us into His
favour and accepts us as righteous persons'.[3] It means 'an acquittal' from all that has separated us from God.[4] It is the pardon of
our sins, after which, in the sight of God we are no longer sinners,
but are clothed with the righteousness of Christ.[5] This is the
starting point for the Christian life, knowing no prerequisites
apart from Christ Himself.[6] As the recipients of God's forgiveness, we enter upon a life that is reconciled to God, where sin no
longer stands between Him and ourselves, 'for since (Christ) has
reconciled us to the Father, our condition is such that He will
show forth more effectually, and daily increase, His favour
towards us'.[7]

We must return here to a subject discussed under our examination of Calvin's insistence on the fact that Christ 'merited' our
redemption, namely, that there is no contradiction between the
free forgiveness of God and the work of Christ. The name of
Christ occurs centrally whenever Calvin speaks of justification:
'A sinner, being received into communion with Christ, is by his
grace reconciled to God, while, being purified by His blood, he
obtains remission of sins.'[8] God's justifying of us and Christ and
His work are not only not contradictory; they are to be identified,

---

[1] *Comm. in 1 Joh.* 3.2, C.R. 83, 331.   [2] *Instit.* III.11.1, C.R. 30, 533.
[3] *Instit.* III.11.2, C.R. 30, 534.   [4] *Instit.* III.11.3, C.R. 30, 535.
[5] *Instit.* III.11.2, C.R. 30, 534.   [6] *Comm. in Heb.* 9.14, C.R. 83, 111-112.
[7] *Comm. in Rom.* 5.8, C.R. 77, 93.   [8] *Instit.* III.17.8, C.R. 30, 596.

in that our justification consists precisely in what God is and has done for us in Christ. 'God alone is the fountain of righteousness, and we are righteous only by a participation in Him; yet because we have been alienated from His righteousness, . . . it is necessary for us to descend to this indirect (*inferius*) remedy, that Christ might justify us by the strength of His death and Resurrection.'[1] Jesus Christ is the way in which God comes to us to justify us.

As we go further and review Calvin's explanation of *how* we are justified by God in Christ, we shall see the relation of justification to incorporation. Justification has the perfect righteousness of Christ as its point of departure.[2] But as we have seen, the righteousness of Christ, His perfect obedience to the will of the Father, is the work of His human nature. 'He justifies us by presenting His own obedience to the Father; and therefore, He does this for us not according to His divine nature, but by reason of the dispensation committed to Him.'[3] It is as man that Christ is our brother and has become our Substitute. Therefore, commenting on Isaiah 53.11, Calvin says: 'He teaches that Christ justifies us, not only as He is God, but also as He is man, for in our flesh He procured righteousness for us. He does not say *the Son*, but *my servant*, that we may not only consider Him as God, but may contemplate His human nature, in which He performed that obedience by which we are acquitted before God.'[4] This distinction is interesting when we remember that the first aspect of the obedience of Christ for Calvin was the Incarnation, the obedience of the *Son of God*. That Calvin should base our justification solely on the *human* obedience of Christ is perhaps an inevitable consequence of his insistence that Christ is our substitute only in His humanity. As a result, the obedience of God the Son, like His humiliation, receives no consequential development.

For Calvin, the substitutionary character of Christ and His perfect obedience in our place is the means of justification. And because, as we have seen, this substitution is the expression of the will of God from all eternity, therefore 'His obedience is accepted for us as if it were our own'.[5] The purpose of His obedience was

---

[1] *Instit.* III.11.8, *C.R.* 30, 539.
[2] 'There is found in (Christ) the exact righteousness of the law, which becomes also ours by imputation.' *Comm. in Rom.* 3.31, *C.R.* 77, 67.
[3] *Instit.* III.11.8, *C.R.* 30, 539.   [4] *Comm. in Isa.* 53.11, *C.R.* 65, 265.
[5] *Instit.* III.11.23, *C.R.* 30, 552.

that it might be carried out in our name.[1] And it becomes effective as a righteousness that is ours when we are incorporated into Christ, having His life and His righteousness as the only ground of our being. If it be said that we remain sinners in ourselves, Calvin answers that, as a result of the substitutionary character of Christ's work and of our incorporation into Him, we have no right to consider ourselves simply as in ourselves, but only in Christ. 'Those whom the Lord has received into his favour (and) incorporated into the communion of Christ, . . . even though they carry sin about within them, yet . . . they are absolved from guilt and condemnation.'[2]

To be justified, then, is to stand before God with the righteousness of Christ Himself. We are 'regarded (by God) as righteous',[3] for the righteousness of Christ is freely accounted as ours.[4] But we must never forget that we have this righteousness, not in ourselves, but in Christ in whom we have our life. 'What is the highest perfection of Christians? . . . Full manhood is found in Christ. For foolish men do not seek their perfection in Christ as they ought. But among us it ought to stand as a principle, that all that is outside of Christ is hurtful and destructive. Whoever is a man *in* Christ, therefore, is in every respect a *perfect* man.'[5] If we have doubts about our righteousness in Christ, then we are doubting His reconciling work, and we do not yet know Christ as our Substitute before the Father.[6] We must learn, therefore, to see ourselves as God sees us: in Christ. God, the author of the substitutionary work of Christ, takes this substitution seriously. 'No sinner can find favour in his right *as a sinner*, or *so long as he is considered as such*.'[7] That is the key to our justification: we are no longer seen in ourselves by God, but only in our Substitute. 'The righteousness of Christ (which, being the only perfect righteousness, is the only one that can bear the divine scrutiny) must be produced on our behalf and judicially presented as in the case of a surety (*sponsorem*).'[8] In His eternal mercy, 'the Father embraces us in Christ, when He invests us

---

[1] '*Et simul notandum est quidquid donorum accepit, ideo magis gratuitum censeri, quia magis ad nos pertinet.*' *Comm. in Ps.* 8.5, C.R. 59, 93.

[2] *Instit.* IV.15.12, C.R. 30, 969.   [3] *Comm. in 2 Cor.* 5.21, C.R. 78, 71.

[4] *Instit.* III.11.16, C.R. 30, 547.   [5] *Comm. in Eph.* 4.13, C.R. 79, 200.

[6] 'Christ is not really known as a Mediator except when all doubt as to our access to God is removed.' *Comm. in Heb.* 4.16, C.R. 83, 55.

[7] *Instit.* III.11.2, C.R. 30, 533.   [8] *Instit.* III.14.12, C.R. 30, 572.

with the righteousness of Christ and accepts it as ours, that by means of it He may treat us as holy, pure, and righteous persons'.[1]

How is it that God accepts Christ's righteousness as ours? God looks at us, but He sees, as it were, not us, but His beloved and righteous Son standing in our place; for Christ 'attracts the eyes (of the Father) to His righteousness, so as to avert them from our sins'.[2] Apart from Christ, we should be lost, for 'no man is loved by God out of Christ'.[3] But, thanks be to God, we are not out of Christ, but in Him, by the power of His Spirit. 'We therefore expect salvation from Him, . . . because, having grafted us into His body, He makes us partakers not only of all His benefits, but also of Himself.'[4] We remain totally dependent on Him as our Substitute, for 'our righteousness is not in ourselves, but in Christ, and all our title to it rests on being partakers of Christ, for we possess all His riches in possessing Him'.[5] Justification rests on substitution made real by incorporation into Christ. 'We do not contemplate Him at a distance out of ourselves, that His righteousness may be imputed to us; but because we have put Him on and are grafted into His body, and because He has deigned to unite us to Himself, therefore we glory in our unity of righteousness with Him.'[6] Substitution is no fiction, but by incorporation it is a reality of the power of God. It is the basis of a wonderful exchange between Christ and ourselves: 'Becoming with us the Son of man, He has made us with Himself the sons of God; descending to the earth, He has prepared for us a way to ascend to Heaven; accepting our mortality, He has conferred on us His immortality; assuming our weakness, He has strengthened us by His power; submitting to our poverty, He has transferred to us His riches; taking on Himself the load of our iniquity with which we were oppressed, He has clothed us with His righteousness.'[7]

Our justification is the fulfilment of God's eternal will for us.[8] His will to exercise His love for us and to receive us to Himself as His children is accomplished in no other way than by His loving Christ and receiving Him in our place. Whence proceeds pardon, but from God's beholding us and all our actions in

---

[1] *Instit.* III.14.12, *C.R.* 30, 572.
[2] *Instit.* II.16.16, *C.R.* 30, 383.
[3] *Instit.* III.2.32, *C.R.* 30, 425.
[4] *Instit.* III.2.24, *C.R.* 30, 418.
[5] *Instit.* III.11.23, *C.R.* 30, 552.
[6] *Instit.* III.11.10, *C.R.* 30, 540.
[7] *Instit.* IV.17.2, *C.R.* 30, 1003.
[8] *Instit.* III.11.16, *C.R.* 30, 547.

Christ?'[1] God is able to love us by loving Christ, and to receive us by receiving Christ. We are loved by the love of the Father for the Son, and we are justified by the Father's pleasure in the righteousness of the Son. 'That love, by which Christ was appointed to be the person in whom we should be freely chosen before we were born and while we were still ruined in Adam, is hidden in the breast of God and far exceeds the capacity of the human mind. True, no man will ever feel that God is kind to him, unless he perceives it is in Christ that God is pacified. But as all relish for the love of God vanishes when Christ is taken away, so we may safely conclude that, since by faith we are grafted into His body, there is no danger of our falling away from the love of God: For this foundation cannot be overturned: that we are loved, *because* the Father has loved (the Son).'[2]

We have reserved to the end the discussion of the role of faith in justification in order to make clear that, for Calvin, we are justified by grace alone, that is, by Christ's incorporation of ourselves into Himself. It would not be a proper presentation of Calvin's teaching to say that we are justified *by* faith, for faith plays only an indirect part in justification. That is, 'the power of justifying belongs not to faith itself, but only as it receives Christ'.[3] Faith, as we have seen, is the sign and witness of incorporation by the Spirit of Christ. It is, therefore, as the *medium* of incorporation that faith plays its role in justification 'by uniting us to Christ, that being made one with Him we may share His righteousness'.[4]

God justifies us in His mercy by grace alone, by uniting us to our Substitute and seeing us in Christ. The role of faith, says Calvin, is that of 'a vessel, for unless we come *empty* with the mouth of our soul open to implore the grace of Christ, we cannot receive Christ'.[5] We have spoken of the gift of faith as the act in which God in Christ reaches out to open men to Himself. This is the same way of conceiving of faith as this analogy of the empty vessel, which presents to Christ nothing but a void. The role of faith in justification is the negative one of existing as the vacuum which Christ fills, witnessing to the fact that our incorporation into Christ is solely the work of His Spirit. With this

---

[1] *Instit.* III.17.10, *C.R.* 30, 597.   [2] *Comm. in Joh.* 17.23, *C.R.* 75, 389.
[3] *Instit.* III.11.7, *C.R.* 30, 538.   [4] *Instit.* III.17.11, *C.R.* 30, 599.
[5] *Instit.* III.11.7, *C.R.* 30, 538.

vacuum, we stand before the mercy of God in Christ. Over against the activity of God's mercy stands the passivity, or better, the receptivity of faith. Faith does not 'procure righteousness for us by its intrinsic merit, as an act of obedience to the divine will'. That would be a positive and false conception of the nature of faith and its role in justification. Rather, it embraces the divine mercy, and offers its emptiness to receive Christ and His righteousness.[1] Faith plays its part in justification by insisting, as it were, that it does *not* justify, and it 'attributes everything to Christ and places no dependence in ourselves'.[2]

Faith remains, however negative its role may be, as a necessary element in reconciliation. Without it we remain closed to Christ. 'The apostle teaches here (Heb. 9.15) the same thing as we find in Romans 3.25, that righteousness and salvation have been procured by the blood of Christ, but that we become partakers of them by faith.'[3] Faith takes its place in the order of justification behind everything else, but it remains a necessary element. 'In our justification, therefore, the efficient cause is the mercy of God; Christ is the matter; the Word with faith is the instrument. Consequently, faith is said to justify, because it is the instrument to receive Christ, in whom righteousness is communicated unto us.'[4] As the God-given openness to receive Christ, faith is the instrument or medium of justification, so that one may properly say that we are justified by grace through faith.

Strictly speaking, then, we are justified by incorporation into Christ. 'Grafted into the death of Christ, we draw from it a secret energy, as the twig does from the root. . . . But let us remember, that we are delivered . . . only by becoming one with Christ, as the twig draws its sap only by growing into one nature (with the tree).'[5] We are restored to righteous fellowship with God by our union with Christ Himself. 'Through the sin of Adam, we are not condemned by mere imputation, as though the punishment of the sin of another were inflicted upon us; but rather, we sustain the punishment of his sin because we are also guilty of his crime, namely, in as much as our nature, being corrupted in him, is held guilty of iniquity before God. But we

---

[1] *Instit.* III.18.10, C.R. 30, 612.   [2] *Instit.* IV.17.42, C.R. 30, 1045.
[3] *Comm. in Heb.* 9.15, C.R. 83, 113.
[4] *Comm. in Rom.* 3.22, C.R. 77, 60. Cf. *Instit.* III.14.17, C.R. 30, 575.
[5] *Comm. in Gal.* 2.20, C.R. 78, 198.

are restored to salvation by the righteousness of Christ in another way; for it is imputed to us, not as though it were within us, but because we possess Christ Himself with all His graces, given unto us by the bountifulness of the Father.'[1]

[1] *Comm. in Rom.* 5.17, C.R. 77, 100.

CHAPTER IX

THE BODY OF CHRIST

1. CHRIST'S BODY

THE central and unifying element in Calvin's teaching about the Incarnation, the Atonement and incorporation is the human body assumed by the Son of God, in which He performed His substitutionary work, and into which He has incorporated us by His Spirit. The reason for this emphasis on the humanity of Christ is that Christ can be in our place only because of the fact that He has taken on our nature. Calvin refers frequently, moreover, to Christ's body in discussing incorporation: we are made His members when we become united to Him. It is necessary, therefore, to review His teaching about the Church as the body of Christ, in order to see what Calvin means when he says that 'Christ is not without us, but dwells within us, and not only adheres to us by an indivisible bond of fellowship, but by a certain wonderful communion unites Himself with us daily more and more into one body, until He becomes altogether one with us'.[1]

It is necessary to begin by emphasizing first of all the words *of Christ*. Calvin points out again and again that the Church is to Christ as a body is to its head: *i.e.* dependent and subordinate. As God loves us by loving the Son, so, in other words, he loves us by loving Christ 'inasmuch as He is the Head of the Church'.[2] And again: 'That love by which the Heavenly Father embraces the Head of the Church He extends to all the members also, so that He loves none but those in Christ.'[3] Although the Church is called the body of Christ, there can be no confusion between Christ and His Church. The relationship of over and under, first and second, is made clear by Calvin's insistence on the bodily Ascension of Christ. This imposes no limitation on the power of our Lord, but it does mean that Christ's body exists at the right

---

[1] *Instit.* III.2.24, *C.R.* 30, 418. [2] *Comm. in Joh.* 15.9, *C.R.* 75, 342.
[3] *Comm. in Joh.* 17.23, *C.R.* 75, 388.

hand of the Father, and not here on earth. 'The word *ascend* denotes a separation of places; but though Christ be absent in body, yet because He is with God, His power, which spreads everywhere, plainly shows His *spiritual presence*.'[1] Since Christ had a real human body, and since there was a Resurrection, so that He remains now as He was then, Ascension means that Christ is bodily in Heaven, although He is with us by the power of His Spirit.[2]

But this very ascended body is the source of all the benefits of Christ that we have, for it is by our union with Christ's body, the instrument of His substitutionary work, that His work is efficacious for us. 'Then only will you find life in Christ when you shall seek the means of life in His flesh.'[3] Participation in the benefits of Christ requires, as we have seen, a participation in Christ Himself, in His flesh and blood.[4] But our connection with Christ is a spiritual one, given to us by the Holy Spirit.[5] Because Christ's body is in Heaven, therefore, and because our union with Him is spiritual, the expression 'the body of Christ', when applied to the Church, cannot be taken as a physical definition, but has all its reality subject to the sovereign freedom of the Spirit of God in Christ. As an expression of the fact that Christians are gathered together into an ordered relationship to God in Jesus Christ, however, the phrase 'the body of Christ' is a fitting description of the Church. 'Truly, out of Christ, what can be perceived in the world but mere ruins? For we are alienated from God by sin; how can we but be wretchedly dispersed and broken? The proper condition of creatures is to keep close to God. Such a gathering together as might bring us back to a regular order, the apostle tells us, has been made in Christ. Gathered into His body, we are united to God and joined to each other.'[6]

When Calvin calls the Church 'the body of Christ', therefore,

---

[1] *Comm. in Joh.* 20.17, *C.R.* 75, 435.

[2] *Instit.* IV.17.16ff, *C.R.* 30, 1015f. Cf. *Comm. in Col.* 3.1, *C.R.* 80, 118.

[3] *Comm. in Joh.* 6.55, *C.R.* 75, 155.   [4] *Instit.* IV.17.9, *C.R.* 30, 1008.

[5] 'In so far as Christ's flesh is quickening and is a heavenly food to nourish souls, in so far as His blood is a spiritual drink and is cleansing, we are not to imagine anything earthly or material in them.' *Comm. in Heb.* 9.11, *C.R.* 83, 110. That is, His body in and of itself is of course material, but with respect to its 'efficacy', *i.e.* what it is for us, that we have solely through the power of the Spirit.

[6] *Comm. in Eph.* 1.10, *C.R.* 79, 151.

he means neither Christ's own body in Heaven, nor a second
body independent of Christ. Nor is the Church likened to just
any body, but to Christ's own body which He assumed in order
to carry out His work in our place, that we might be grafted
into Him in a unity that restores us to fellowship with God. 'To
understand correctly what was intended by saying that Christ
and the Father are one, we must take care not to deprive Christ
of His office of Mediator, but rather consider Him as the Head
of the Church, and unite Him with His members. Thus will the
chain of thought be preserved, that in order to prevent the unity
of the Son with the Father from being fruitless and unavailing,
its powers must be diffused through the whole body of believers.
Hence too, we infer that we are one with Christ, not because He
pours his substance into us, but because, by the power of His
Spirit, He imparts to us His life and all the blessings which He
has received from the Father.'[1] It is clear from this passage that
when Calvin calls the Church the body of which Christ is the
Head, he is expressing the efficacy of Christ's character as our
Substitute. The Church is the body of Christ because of the fact
that Christ exists for us and in our place.

2. THE CHURCH AS THE BODY OF CHRIST

All that has been said about substitution and incorporation
makes it almost inevitable that Calvin's doctrine of the Church
should have its foundation in the person and work of Christ.
This fact is perhaps not immediately apparent when we turn to
Book IV of the *Institutes*, where Calvin begins his presentation
of ecclesiology, for his first statements about the Church have to
do with the necessity for membership in the Church. 'There is,'
he says, 'no other way of entrance into life' except through the
all-too-visible Church.[2] Union with her 'retains us in the fellowship of God',[3] and she is the way that God has given us of
approaching Him, thus 'accommodating Himself to our capacity'.[4]
Thus, 'the Church is the mother of all who have Him for their
Father',[5] for to her alone belongs the benefit of forgiveness of
sins.[6] All this is so, however, because the Church is the body and
the bride of Christ. '*Hence it follows* that a departure from the

---

[1] *Comm. in Joh.* 17.21, C.R. 75, 387.
[2] *Instit.* IV.1.4, C.R. 30, 749.
[3] *Instit.* IV.1.3, C.R. 30, 748.
[4] *Instit.* IV.1.1, C.R. 30, 745.
[5] *Instit.* IV.1.1, C.R. 30, 746.
[6] *Instit.* IV.1.22, C.R. 30, 763.

Church is a renunciation of God and Christ', for it would be disastrous to 'violate the marriage that the only-begotten Son of God has condescended to form with us'.[1] The necessity for membership in the Church shows that, for Calvin, ecclesiology is based on Christology. Commenting on Isaiah 54.1, he says: 'After having spoken of the death of Christ, he turns with good reason to the Church, that we may feel more deeply within ourselves what is the value and efficacy of His death. For we cannot behold it in Christ if He be considered by Himself; therefore we must come to His body, which is the Church, because Christ suffered for it and not for Himself. And this is the order observed in our confession of faith; for, after having professed that we believe in Christ, who suffered and was crucified for us, we add that we believe in the Church, which flowed, as it were, from His side. Accordingly, having spoken of the death, Resurrection, and triumph of Christ, Isaiah properly comes down to the Church, which ought never to be separated from her Head.'[2]

The Church, 'which flows from the side of Christ', is derived totally from Him. Commenting on the text, 'For we are members of his body, of his flesh and of his blood', Calvin says: 'This is no exaggeration, but the simple truth.'[3] Again: 'The spiritual unity that we have with Christ belongs not merely to the soul, but also to the body, so that we are flesh of His flesh, etc. (Eph. 5.30). Otherwise the hope of a resurrection were weak, if our connection were not of that nature—full and complete.'[4] Having heard what Calvin has to say about Christ as our Substitute and our incorporation into Him, we find, upon coming to consider the Church, that we have already heard most of what he has to say about the Church. That is, to speak of the Church as the body of Christ is to speak in other words about incorporation into our Substitute. Commenting on 1 Cor. 12.12, Calvin says: 'It is a passage full of special consolation, in that he calls the Church *Christ*; for Christ confers upon us this honour: that He is willing to be esteemed and recognized, not merely in Himself, but also in His members. Hence (Paul) says elsewhere (Eph. 1.23) that the Church is His *completion*, as though He would be incomplete

[1] *Instit.* IV.1.10, C.R. 30, 755.
[2] *Comm. in Isa.* 54.1, C.R. 65, 268-269.
[3] *Comm. in Eph.* 5.30, C.R. 79, 225.
[4] *Comm. in* 1 *Cor.* 6.15, C.R. 77, 398.

if separated from His members.'[1] We should be inventing an inferior Christ were we to try to conceive of Him apart from His substitutionary character. Again, where Paul speaks of the Galatians as having put on Christ, Calvin says: 'He means that they are so grafted into Him, that in the presence of God they bear the name and character of Christ and are considered in Him rather than in themselves.'[2]

To understand the Church as the body of Christ is to see in Christ those for whom the Son of God became a Substitute, and in whose name He stands now before the Father. The Father wills to see the Church only in Christ, and in the obedience of faith we are called to understand ourselves as He understands us. The Church, acknowledging that she lives by virtue of her Substitute, should confess herself as the body of Christ, not as a confession of her own character, but as a confession of the reality of the substitutionary character of Christ. When Calvin calls us the body of Christ, he is saying more about Christ than he is about ourselves.

Because we are the body of Christ—that is to say, because we are those for whom He is in all eternity the true Substitute before the Father, into whom we have been incorporated by His Spirit —what is said of him is applicable to us, and even what is said of us must apply, in a sense, to Him. Thus where the Bible speaks of the sinlessness of Christ, Calvin can say that it speaks 'not of Christ personally, but of His whole body'.[3] Commenting on Psalm 40.7, and the application of this to Christ by the author of Hebrews (Heb. 10.5), Calvin says: 'As to (his applying this passage to) the person of Christ, the solution is simple, for David did not speak in his own name only, but has shown in general what belongs to all the children of God. But in bringing up the subject of the community of the Church, it was necessary that he should refer to the Head itself. It is no objection that a little later (David, in the name of the Church, and thus also in Christ's name) imputes to his own sins the miseries which he endures, for it is by no means an uncommon thing to find our errors, by a mode of expression not strictly correct, transferred to Christ.'[4]

[1] *Comm. in* 1 *Cor.* 12.12, *C.R.* 77, 501.
[2] *Comm. in Gal.* 3.27, *C.R.* 78, 222.
[3] *Comm. in* 1 *Joh.* 3.5, *C.R.* 83, 333.
[4] *Comm. in Ps.* 40.7, *C.R.* 59, 412.

The Church is the body of Christ. But Christ existed first in a condition of shame and humility, and only later, not visible to our sight, in a condition of glory. Since the Church is His body, the condition of the Church must be that of its Head. This, according to Calvin, is the teaching that lies behind the apocalyptic passage of Mark 13 and the Synoptic parallels. Because the disciples expected Christ to begin His messianic Kingdom in glory on earth, it was necessary to warn them that the Church, following its Lord, must begin in lowliness. 'They received an answer very different from what they had expected, for whereas they were eager for triumph, as if they had already served their enlistment, Christ exorts them to long patience. . . . By these words He gives warning that His Church, so long as its pilgrimage in this world shall last, will be exposed to these evils.'[1] He began in humility; the Cross came before the Resurrection. Consequently, the Church must begin in the same way: as the crucified body of Christ. Thus the very weakness and smallness of the Church, far from being a problem to Calvin, is grounded theologically on the person and work of Christ. 'The reason why God defers the manifestation of our glory is this: *because* Christ is not manifested in the power of His Kingdom.'[2]

But Christ has risen from the dead, although His glory is not seen by human eyes. So the Church also has a glory that is not yet revealed except to eyes of faith. 'The weak and frail condition of the Church ought not to lead us to conclude that it is dying, but rather to expect the immortal glory for which the Lord prepares His people by the Cross and afflictions, for what Paul says about the individual members must be fulfilled in the whole body: that if the outer man is decayed, the inner man is renewed day by day (2 Cor. 4.16).'[3] We have a glory already, but we have it, as the body of Christ, in our Head. 'Certainly in ourselves, our salvation is the object of hope and still hidden; yet in Christ we possess a blessed immortality and glory. . . . So far, it does not appear in the members, but only in the Head, yet in consequence of the secret union, it belongs truly to the members.'[4] It is Christ Himself, the Head and not the members, who deter-

---

[1] *Comm. in Matth.* 24.4, C.R. 73, 650. Cf. *in Matth.* 16.20, C.R. 73, 479.
[2] *Comm. in* 1 *Joh.* 3.2, C.R. 83, 330.
[3] *Comm. in Matth.* 24.32, C.R. 73, 670.
[4] *Comm. in Eph.* 2.6, C.R. 79, 164.

mines what is the truth about His body. What *He* is, it is, and not the reverse. Because He is in Heaven, we can never be at home in the world, for we are *His* body. 'Accordingly, as Christ is in Heaven, in order that we may be joined together with Him, it is necessary that we should dwell in spirit apart from the world.'[1] Thus the Church is visible, as the Cross is visible to the eyes of the world, but that which makes the Church to be different from any other society, that which constitutes her glory, is invisible, as the glory of the Resurrection is hidden from natural sight. '(Paul) teaches that our life is hid not only in the opinion of the world, but *even from our own* sight; for this is the true and necessary trial of our hope, that being surrounded, so to speak, with death, we may seek life somewhere else than in the world.'[2] The Church is not only constituted by the substitutionary work of Christ; she lives in every moment and element of her existence by that substitution, so that her only life and glory is the life and glory of Jesus Christ.

The Church is the body of Christ; she is called, therefore, to perfect submission and obedience to her Head. 'The body, it is true, has its nerves, its joints and ligaments; but all these things derive their strength solely from the Head, so that the whole binding of them together is from that source. What, then, must be done? The constitution of the body will be in a right state if the Head alone, which supplies the several members with everything that they have, is allowed, without any hindrance, to have the pre-eminence.'[3] To depart from this obedience were to cut oneself off from the body, and therefore to cease to be the Church.[4] To be the body of Christ means to be totally dependent on Him.[5] '(Paul) teaches that it is Christ alone who has authority to govern the Church, that it is He alone to whom believers ought to pay attention, and on whom alone the unity of the body depends.'[6]

By making us members of His body, which is another way of saying, by standing in our place as our Substitute and by making this substitution effective by incorporation, Christ fulfils His eternal purpose and therefore realizes His own existence. 'This is the highest honour of the Church, that until He is united to us,

---

[1] *Comm. in Phil.* 3.20, C.R. 80, 56.   [2] *Comm. in Col.* 3.3, C.R. 80, 119.
[3] *Comm. in Col.* 2.19, C.R. 80, 113.   [4] *Comm. in Eph.* 1.22, C.R. 79, 159.
[5] 'The Papists, inventing for us a Church separated from Christ the Head, leave us a maimed and mutilated body.' *Comm. in Matth.* 19.6, C.R. 73, 529.
[6] *Comm. in Col.* 1.18, C.R. 80, 86-87.

K

the Son of God reckons Himself in some measure imperfect. What consolation it is for us to hear that not until we are with Him does he possess all His parts or wish to be regarded as complete!'[1] To prevent our thinking that we have something from ourselves to add to Christ, Calvin points out that when Paul calls the Church 'the fullness of him', he adds the words 'who fills all in all', 'lest anyone suppose that any defect would exist in Christ if He were separated from us. His wish to be filled and in some sense made perfect in us arises from no defect or need, for all that is good in ourselves or in any of the creatures He performs Himself, and His goodness appears the more in making us out of nothing, in order that He might in turn also live in us.'[2] There is no external necessity, least of all from our side, by which Christ might regard Himself as unfulfilled in Himself alone. The necessity by which He refuses to exist in and of Himself, and wills to exist in our place as our Substitute is the necessity of His own love and mercy. God in Jesus Christ, in His eternal will and being, is *pro nobis*. That is why Christ 'will no more suffer His faithful people to be severed from Him than His limbs to be mutilated and torn in pieces'.[3] Because Christ is in His very being our Substitute, we must remember when we speak of Him that we are also speaking about the Church, 'which ought never to be separated from Christ'.[4]

The Church is the body of Christ, therefore we are all members in the same body. Because He has made Himself our brother, He has constituted us brothers of one another. 'The saints are united in the fellowship of Christ on this condition: that whatever benefits God confers upon them they should mutually share with one another.'[5] Here is, for Calvin, the theological basis of the unity of the Church: 'All the elect of God are so connected with each other in Christ that, as they depend upon one Head, so they grow up together as into one body, . . . being called not only to the same inheritance of eternal life, but also to a participation in one God and Christ.'[6] This is the principal practical consequence of the teaching that the Church is the body of Christ. This is what distinguishes the fellowship of Christians and the character of the Christian community from every other possible form of

---

[1] *Comm. in Eph.* 1.23, C.R. 79, 159.   [2] *Comm. in Eph.* 1.23, C.R. 79, 160.
[3] *Instit.* IV.1.3, C.R. 30, 748.   [4] *Comm. in Isa.* 53.8, C.R. 65, 261.
[5] *Instit.* IV.1.3, C.R. 30, 747-748.   [6] *Instit.* IV.1.2, C.R. 30, 747.

human society, 'for we are not a mere civil society, but, being grafted into Christ's body, we are truly members one of another'.[1] The word *body* when applied to the Church has a very different meaning from when it is used of any other group, for we are the body *of Christ*: 'It is usual for any society of men or congregation to be called a body, as one city constitutes a body, and so one senate, and one people. . . . Among Christians, however, the case is very different, for they do not constitute a mere political body, but they are the spiritual and secret body of Christ.'[2] The unity of the Church is not based upon ourselves or upon our decision, but is based upon the oneness of Christ, for as He has but one body, so we, being in Him, must also be one.[3] Being reconciled to God in Him, we are also, by that very fact, reconciled to one another.[4] This is the reason why Calvin has been able to stress the necessity for membership in the Church, 'for unless we are united with all the other members under Christ our Head, we can have no hope of the future inheritance'.[5] And this is also the reason for the unity within the Church, for, because God in Christ is one, so the Church is one, for 'God is not inconsistent with Himself. Therefore we cannot but be united in one body.'[6]

Finally, within the unity of the body of Christ, every member has his own place and function. Thus there are three things to learn from the biblical teaching that the Church is the body of Christ:[7] that the Church must be subject to her Head, that union with Christ involves union with one another, and that, under Christ, we must be for each other, as He is for us, not seeking our own individual advantage, but only the good of the whole of the body. On this last point Calvin says, commenting on Ephesians 4.16: 'Lastly, he shows that by love the Church is edified. . . . This means that no increase is useful which does not correspond with the whole of the body. That man is mistaken who desires his own separate growth. For what good would it do a leg or an arm if it should grow to enormous size, or if the mouth be spread wider, except to be weighed down by the harmful swelling? In like manner, if we wish to be considered in Christ, let no man be

---

[1] *Comm. in* 1 *Cor.* 12.27, *C.R.* 77, 505.
[2] *Comm. in* 1 *Cor.* 12.12, *C.R.* 77, 501.
[3] *Instit.* IV.17.38, *C.R.* 30, 1041.   [4] *Comm. in* 1 *Cor.* 1.13, *C.R.* 77, 316.
[5] *Instit.* IV.1.2, *C.R.* 30, 747.   [6] *Comm. in Eph.* 4.6, *C.R.* 79, 192.
[7] *Comm. in Eph.* 4.16, *C.R.* 79, 203.

anything for himself, but let us all be whatever we are for the benefit of each other.'[1]

At this point Calvin's teaching raises a question that is related to the other questions already discussed. If the Church is the body of Christ, and if Christ offers Himself to all men as the one who suffered and rose again in the place of all men, if Christ is Himself *pro nobis*, then ought we not to hear from Calvin that the Church as Christ's body exists for the sake of others and not for itself? The consequential conclusion to the teaching that the Church is Christ's body would be the sending of the Church into the world for the sake of the world. Calvin, however, speaks of the Church, as distinguished from the world, as vessels sanctified to honour,[2] and as being exalted by a 'special privilege above the whole world'.[3] We grant that the Church has the privilege of knowing Christ and what He has done in the place of all men, but does it have this knowledge for itself only, or does it have this knowledge also for those who are not as yet aware of what God has done in Christ? Christ's body was assumed in the place of all men, as we have seen, and this body is for us the source of life. 'The flesh of Christ is like a rich and inexhaustible fountain, which receives the life flowing from the divinity and conveys it to us.' When Calvin goes on to say that 'the Church is the body of Christ' on the basis of '*His* entire union both of body and spirit with us',[4] is he not suggesting that the Church is taken up into the substitutionary character of Christ, existing in a representative capacity which reflects the substitutionary character of Him who gave Himself for all men, and therefore existing for the sake of those not in the Church? Perhaps because of the way in which Calvin understood Christ's own substitutionary character, this remains only a suggestion which he did not develop. Surely this could have been the point of departure for the doctrine of the mission of the Church, a subject which plays only a minor role in Calvin's doctrine of the Church.

We have followed the line of Calvin's doctrine of Reconciliation, from the person of Christ, through the work of Christ and incorporation by the Spirit through faith, to the Church, and have seen the consistency of the whole. Consequently, our questions raised concerning his understanding of the person of Christ—the

---

[1] *Comm. in Eph* 4.16, C.R. 79, 205.   [2] *Instit.* IV.1.17, C.R. 30, 760.
[3] *Comm. in Joh.* 14.17, C.R. 75, 329.   [4] *Instit.* IV.17.9, C.R. 30, 1009.

impassability of His divine nature, and the sinless condition of His human nature—led in turn to questions about the division of labour in the two natures of Christ, and about Calvin's insistence that only as man is Christ our Substitute. These then formed the basis of our major question about the way in which Calvin understood the work of Christ as being the reality of salvation, which led to the question about the role of faith in reconciliation. Out of respect for the consequentialness of Calvin's theology we would point out that our question about the mission of the Church is based on the criticism we have made all along, and goes back ultimately to the questions raised in Part I.

3. THE SACRAMENTS AS SIGNS OF INCORPORATION

Along with the proclamation of the good news that God has taken our place in Jesus Christ and incorporated us into the body of Christ, Christ has also given to His Church the Sacraments, that we may have a visible form also of this proclamation. 'The office of the Sacraments is precisely the same as that of the Word of God, which is to offer and present Christ to us and, in Him, the treasures of His heavenly grace.'[1] We do not intend to give in any sense a complete review of Calvin's doctrine of the Sacraments, but only a brief outline of what he has to say on this matter as it relates to our subject of the substitutionary character of Christ and of our incorporation into Him.

It must be said first that for Calvin the Sacraments are never to be considered in isolation from that which they are intended to convey. 'God acts by the sign in such a way that its whole efficacy depends upon His Spirit. Nothing more is attributed to the sign than to be an inferior organ, utterly useless in itself, except in so far as it derives its power from another source.'[2] Therefore, we must not ascribe to the Sacraments 'the praise of those benefits which are only conferred upon us by Christ alone and by the agency of the Holy Spirit, who makes us partakers of Christ Himself by the instrumentality of the external signs which invite us to Christ.'[3] On the other hand, we must not make the mistake of thinking that the signs are empty and have no value. Christ Himself and all His benefits 'are presented to us'[4] in the

---

[1] *Instit.* IV.14.17, *C.R.* 30, 953.   [2] *Comm. in Eph.* 5.26, *C.R.* 79, 223.
[3] *Instit.* IV.14.16, *C.R.* 30, 953.   [4] *Instit.* IV.14.23, *C.R.* 30, 959.

Sacraments. We are to understand the Sacraments as signs, therefore, but as valid and trustworthy signs.

The first of these signs is that of baptism, which is a sign of our incorporation into Christ, and, therefore, into His body, the Church. 'Baptism is a sign of initiation, by which we are admitted into the society of the Church, in order that, being incorporated into Christ, we may be numbered among the children of God.'[1] It is a sign, also, of our purification, and of our mortification and new life in Christ,[2] but this is so because it is, in the first place, a witness to our incorporation. Baptism 'affords us the certain testimony', Calvin says, 'that we are not only grafted into the life and death of Christ, but are so united to Christ Himself as to be partakers of all His benefits'.[3] As a sign of this reality, it is connected with the reality itself, not only in meaning but also in God's action. 'When Paul says that we are washed by baptism, his meaning is that God employs it for declaring to us that we are washed, and at the same time performs what it represents. If the truth—or, which is the same thing, the exhibition of the truth—were not connected with (baptism), it would be improper to say that baptism is the washing of the soul. At the same time, we must beware of ascribing to the sign or to the minister what belongs to God alone.'[4] Baptism, therefore, represents a fact. Those who accept baptism accept the fact that they are incorporated into Christ. Paul 'makes no boast of any false splendour as belonging to the Sacrament, but at the same time he calls attention to the actual fact represented by the outward ceremony'.[5] The Sacrament of baptism, therefore, is the outward sign of the reality of our being incorporated into Christ by the Spirit, a reality that accompanies but is not identical with the sign.[6] The exact relationship between the sign and the reality is not part of our subject, and in these passages we would call attention only to the fact that the Sacraments find their place in Calvin's theology as the trustworthy signs of our incorporation into our Substitute. Because the work of Christ in our place was in obedience to the eternal will of the Father, and because we are incorporated into Christ by the Spirit, therefore we are bap-

---

[1] *Instit.* IV.15.1, *C.R.* 30, 962.   [2] *Instit.* IV.15.1, 5, *C.R.* 30, 962, 964.
[3] *Instit.* IV.15.6, *C.R.* 30, 965.   [4] *Comm. in Eph.* 5.26, *C.R.* 79, 223.
[5] *Comm. in Gal.* 3.27, *C.R.* 78, 222.
[6] *Comm. in 1 Cor.* 12.13, *C.R.* 77, 501-502.

tized in the name of the triune God. 'All the gifts of God which are presented in baptism are found in Christ alone. Yet it cannot be but that he who baptizes into Christ at the same time invokes the name of the Father and of the Spirit. For we have purification in His blood because our merciful Father, in His incomparable goodness, wishing to receive us in His favour, has appointed this Mediator between us, to conciliate His favour to us. But we receive regeneration from His death and Resurrection when we are endued with a new and spiritual nature by the Spirit of sanctification.'[1] Baptism, then, is a sign that points back to all that we have been saying, and is a witness to the reality of our union with Christ.

As a continual support to our knowledge that we have our existence in Christ our Substitute, we have been given a second sign: the Sacrament of the Lord's Supper. It is a 'symbol and pledge' of 'our union with Christ'.[2] 'Because this mystery of the secret union of Christ with believers is incomprehensible by nature, (God) exhibits a figure and image of it in visible signs peculiarly adapted to our capacity, and, as it were, by giving tokens and pledges, makes it as certain to us as if we beheld it with our eyes.'[3] The Lord's Supper 'affords us a testimony that we are incorporated into one body with Christ, so that whatever is His we are allowed to call ours'.[4] The way in which Calvin understands the Lord's Supper as a sign of incorporation is indicative of his whole treatment of this Sacrament. He does not fasten upon the words, 'This is my body', in an attempt to find the whole of his teaching there, but sees them always in a wider context. So, in explaining how this Sacrament witnesses to incorporation, he says: 'The body, therefore, which was once offered for our salvation, we are commanded to take and eat, that seeing ourselves made partakers of it, we may certainly conclude that the power of that life-giving death will be efficacious within us.'[5] And again: 'As He has only one body, of which He makes us all partakers, it follows necessarily that by such participation we are all made one body also; and this union is represented by the bread which is exhibited in the Sacrament.'[6] Because Calvin takes this wide perspective in seeing the Lord's Supper as a

---

[1] *Instit.* IV.15.6, C.R. 30, 965.   [2] *Comm. in Eph.* 5.29, C.R. 79, 225.
[3] *Instit.* IV.17.1, C.R. 30, 1002.   [4] *Instit.* IV.17.2, C.R. 30, 1003.
[5] *Instit.* IV.17.1, C.R. 30, 1003.   [6] *Instit.* IV.17.38, C.R. 30, 1041.

representation of our incorporation into our Substitute, whereby we are constituted one body in Him, we have no need here to enter into a review of what he has to say about the controversy over the meaning of the words, 'This is my body'. For, as Calvin says, 'the principal object of the Sacrament is not to present to us the body of Christ, simply and without any deeper consideration, but rather to confirm that promise where He declares that His flesh is meat indeed and His blood drink indeed.'[1] We must remember, Calvin tells us, that Christ is the bread of life first of all in Himself and His work; He does not first become the bread of life in the Sacrament.[2] He gave His body 'to be made bread, when He surrendered it to be crucified for the redemption of the world; He gives it daily when by the word of the Gospel He offers it to us that we may partake of it as crucified, when He confirms that offer by the sacred mystery of the Supper, when He accomplished internally that which He signifies externally'.[3]

Calvin's presentation of his own position on this Sacrament is a short and powerful summary of all that he has had to say about the Incarnation, the Atonement by Christ's substitutionary work, and our incorporation into Him to be one body with all believers. The Lord's Supper, in Calvin's theology, is the representation of this event of our reconciliation, whereby, in the power of the Holy Spirit, we are taken up into communion with our Lord and feed on Him as the source of our life.[4] By presenting us with the tangible sign of our dependence on the body of our Lord who was offered for us in our place, the Sacrament of the Lord's Supper is a witness of our incorporation into Him.

Calvin's teaching about the Sacraments helps us to see that His doctrine of the Church is a reflection of His Christology, and a reflection of His teaching about the substitutionary character of Christ and our incorporation into Him. Because Christ became our Substitute, we have our reconciliation in Him, in His body. Because He remains our Substitute and stands before the Father in our place, we have our life from Him and live in total dependence upon Him, as a body depends on its head. Because our only life is the life that He lives in our place with the Father, the Church may live in the world in weakness with the confidence that its eschatological hope is not in vain. The teaching that the

---

[1] *Instit.* IV.17.4, *C.R.* 30, 1004.   [2] *Instit.* IV.17.5, *C.R.* 30, 1005.
[3] Ibid.   [4] *Instit.* IV.17.8-11, *C.R.* 30, 1007-1010.

Church is the body of Christ, and that the Sacraments witness to our incorporation into Him, therefore does not present any new departures in Calvin's theology, but is the inevitable consequence and reflection of his teaching that God has dealt with man, and continues to deal with him, in the way in which he exists in Jesus Christ.

CONCLUSION

ALVIN'S teaching has led us from the doctrine of the person of Christ as the One who took our place, in whom God dealt with all men, through the doctrine of the work of Christ in our place, His perfect righteousness and His death and Resurrection in our place and therefore for us, to the doctrine of Christ's incorporation of us into Himself by His Spirit, and the consequences of this incorporation in the Christian life within His body. We have also presented the inner problems of this teaching and have now arrived at a position from which we may ask what are the implications of what we have learned from Calvin for the theology of the Church today.

In Part I we were concerned with Calvin's understanding of the person of Christ, as Son of God, as man, and as the incarnate Son of God. If it was not already clear from our presentation of Calvin's teaching throughout this study, it became quite evident in the development of the inner problems within that teaching that the understanding of the Incarnation is determinative for the doctrine of Reconciliation. What is said about the Incarnation cannot but determine what will be said all the way through a theological work that makes any claim to being orderly. This is so, not because theology as a science has a predetermined logic or basic laws of its own development, but because that event is determinative within the design and will of God. Theology, in expounding the biblical witness to this event, must follow the lead of the reality of which it speaks, and what Calvin said about the Incarnation determined what was to follow. Must not the same be said of contemporary theology?

In presenting the doctrine of the person of Christ, Calvin has followed the traditional lines as originally established in the Chalcedonian formula and as expressed in the so-called Athenasian Creed. We saw Calvin leaning upon the Church Fathers, from Irenaeus on, and there can be no doubt that Calvin was expressing the orthodox position. Yet we saw a problem develop here that had many ramifications. The issue presented to us might

140

be expressed in this way: are we to regard the Incarnation of God the Son, of which the doctrine of the two natures of Christ is the exposition, as the highest expression of revelation, or are we to regard it as a revelation that is not only supreme, but also normative, in that it is so complete that we have no reason and no right to look elsewhere for our understanding of the nature and will of God? It seems certain that Calvin meant to take up the second position. He meant to see Christ as the normative and sufficient revelation of God. If theology today has this same good intention, can it be more consistent than Calvin was in standing by it? Calvin's understanding of the divine nature of Christ is constantly threatened, as we have seen, by a concept of God as impassible Being which he inherited from the whole history of theology, from Irenaeus on, a concept that does not seem to be derived from the Cross or from the Christ who is our Lord only as He is the Crucified One. An incursion of human concepts into the realm of faith is always possible so long as theologians and Christians remain in this world and therefore ever in danger of being of this world, although it is going too far to speak of a second source of revelation in Calvin. But because of the clarity with which he presents the orthodox Christology, his teaching also reveals the dangers that lie in wait for us here and gives us warning of the necessity for careful obedience to the biblical witness of Jesus Christ as the fullness of God's self-revelation.

The subject of our central section, Part II, was the work of Christ. There can be no more accurate way of summing up what we found here than to refer to our title of this study and the title of this central section: Christ in our place. As we have seen, the whole of Calvin's theology turns about this centre. Here is the point from which the rest of his theology is to be understood. There is no competition for this central place between the doctrine of the Incarnation and the doctrine of the Atonement, for, properly understood, they are but two aspects of the one reality of God's saving action that took place in Christ, two aspects of God's grace, and we found that Calvin maintains the oneness of these two aspects. Christ does not exist apart from His work, nor has His work any meaning apart from the fact that it is *His* work. This oneness became clear to us through paying particular attention to the representative or substitutionary character of Christ in His work as Calvin has presented it. We found that this substitutionary character was not simply one among other things that could or should be said about Christ, not some special concern that Calvin wanted to emphasize and add to the general understanding of Christ. On the contrary, we found that if one were to say 'Jesus Christ' with Calvin, one was already saying 'Jesus Christ in our place'. Grounded in Himself, in His person and the whole nature of His work, this substitutionary character is essential to the understanding of Christ.

At a time when the Church is full of many 'theories' of the Atonement, we have something to learn here. That a man of Calvin's calibre and with his knowledge of Scripture—the Old as well as the New Testament—should see in the Bible one clear and consistent picture of the precise nature of the Atonement should give us pause. The adjectives 'penal' and 'substitutionary' have received harsh treatment in many 'theories' of the Atonement in modern times, Friedrich Schleiermacher being one of their biggest opponents. We have been asked by others to look at this as only one of many theories of the Atonement that have come down through the history of theology. Be that as it may, the question remains: has not Calvin seen better than many of us today? That is, has he not in fact picked up the central line of the biblical witness to the work of Christ?

It is odd that a so-called penal-substitutionary doctrine of the Atonement should be thought of as 'objective'. There is an element of truth in such a designation, of course. Calvin shows us that a fair reading of the Bible must insist that this was done for us while we were yet enemies of God and dead in our sins. Yet although it is 'objective' in that it was done outside of ourselves, it was not done without us. We were there, not by our doing but by the sovereign decision of God who dealt with us there in this one Man. Calvin leaves little room for talking about an objective-subjective division in this way, for both of these designations are subsumed under the central fact of the substitutionary character of Christ and His work. He is our representative not because of some general category of humanity that in itself binds Him to us, but because God in the free and merciful exercise of His love chose to come down to us and to be our brother and as such our representative. In Christ, the objective-subjective distinction is overcome by nothing less than God's free decision of grace.

But we found that Calvin brings in an objective-subjective distinction in another way, for there remains a great *if* over the whole of Christ's work, a condition that must still be fulfilled before we can say with the Fourth Gospel, τετέλεσται. Christ's work, in itself, remains for Calvin an unfulfilled possibility. Our question to Calvin on this point, however, is also directed to ourselves and the Church today: are we to say no more than that of the work of Christ? Is Christ only a great possibility for the world, not in Himself the great reality for the world? In what sense are we to call Christ the foundation of our faith and the ultimate determination of our existence and the existence of every human being?

Probably the most basic problem that came to light in this central part, however, was the relation of Christ and His work to the very nature of God, the relation between the way God is in Himself to the way He reveals Himself to be. This question came up in its sharpest form under the meaning of the glory of God. Here too Calvin has left us a problem to be pondered today. If we do not remain absolutely consistent with the New Testament insistence that Christ is the fullness of revelation, the revelation of the very nature of God, the whole of our faith stands in danger. But when that self-revelation of God in all His glory is a revelation of humility, are we not asked to learn that the glory of God is something quite different from our conceptions of glory? Have we a right to look anywhere else than to Christ in order to learn what is the glory and the power and the love of God? It is true that God's ways and thoughts are not our ways and thoughts, but just how different they are we must learn at the foot of the Cross. The traditional concept of God that has dominated the history of Christian doctrine can be accepted only in so far as it conforms to the biblical witness to *this* revelation.

The importance of what was established in the central part of our study became increasingly clear as we tried to see to what extent Calvin could be understood from this centre in those areas covered by the remaining and longest part of his *Institutes*. It became evident in Part III that we were in the realm of a further development of the points already established. And yet we could not help noticing a wall dividing the way already travelled and the path now opening up before us. It could not be denied, of course, that we *do* stand before a certain wall, a miracle of God, when we try to understand and explain how it is that we happen to be Christians. That there should be a Church, men called out of the world to be witnesses in the world of God's work in Christ, men who have been taken up into this work which is the essential determination of their existence, that is all far from being self-evident. But the question is simply whether Calvin's understanding of God's breaking down of this wall by the Holy Spirit is adequate. In this area, our original question to Calvin concerning the involvement of God in the Incarnation in terms of the doctrine of the two natures of Christ became increasingly serious. It did so because Calvin himself insists that the Holy Spirit is none other than the Spirit of Jesus Christ. By stressing his Christological foundation at every point, Calvin calls us back at every step of the way to re-examine the doctrine of the person of Christ and His work in our place, and no question that we have felt obliged to raise in this third Part does not have its prior form in the questions raised at the beginning of our study. We are forced to reconsider continually the precise way in which Calvin understands the work of Christ as the reality of the world's reconciliation to God, a reality which is actualized, however, for any individual by the work of the Holy Spirit. We are left with this question to consider: How are the work of Christ and our being brought to the knowledge of Him and His work by His Spirit to be related to each other? We raised the question in its sharpest form by suggesting that Calvin's teaching at least comes near to defining the relationship as that of a possibility and its realization. If universalism is to be avoided, so also is any teaching that fails to do full justice to the biblical witness, which recognizes, in the power of the Holy Spirit who alone can awaken us to this knowledge, that Christ is in Himself the full reality of our salvation and therefore the content of what we have to proclaim to all men as truly *good* news for them as well as for us.

The implications of this study in Calvin's theology are fairly clear for the Church today, or at least they could be if we are willing to learn from him. The most obvious is the importance of and, in fact, the necessity for a Christological foundation for theology at every step of the way, and therefore the danger of trying to discuss any doctrine apart from this foundation. But Calvin also directs us to consider *how* we make Christ the centre of our thoughts, for all our critical questions might be summed up as pointing to one fact that dominates the way in which Christ is central for Calvin. That fact is the existence of clear boundaries that define the area within which all that Christ is and does is determinative. That is to say, if we limit ourselves to the concern for the relationship between Christ and the Christians, we find ourselves with Calvin within a situation that is in itself complete and satisfactory theologically and whose foundation in Christ is solid. But as soon as one looks out over the limits of this situation and raises the question about 'the world' or the so-called 'reprobate', one realizes that perhaps the very completeness of this inner circle is not all that it should be. Christology does indeed determine all that takes place within this precisely defined circle, but what defines and fixes the circle itself? Has Christology also determined the extent of its own application? Is it this same Jesus Christ on whom rest the Church and every Christian who has set the limits to his own efficacy? We have tried to avoid the question of predestination in our study, but it is clear that the whole line of our critique leads back inevitably to this problem.

If we are to learn from Calvin, then we must see he is right in seeing the σῶμα χριστοῦ as the central fact that theology has to consider. The Incarnation, the work of Christ, Christ as our Substitute in all this, the incorporation of men into Christ, their justification and sanctification in Christ, the Church as Christ's body, all these turn about one phrase and one reality: the body of Christ. Only predestination does not share this common centre for Calvin. But if we set aside the question of predestination as being to one side of, if behind, our immediate concern in this study, we have something to learn from the fact that Calvin makes the body of Christ the dogmatic key to his theology. This possibility to learn from further study of Calvin is especially clear today because of the fact that the World Council of Churches, in its Lund report on the nature of the Church, finds itself approaching a Christological foundation for the understanding of the Church. If there is to be a growing ecumenical unity in this area, it can only come by forcing ourselves to examine more closely what Paul means by speaking of the Church as Christ's body, and, what is more important, by understanding this designation of the Church, as Calvin does, by taking it back to the person and work of Christ Himself. This is the service that Calvin can still render us today, if we are willing to let him. We may or may not agree with him in all that he says, but we would do well to listen in all seriousness to the *way* in which he comes to his conclusions. If we do that, then we will at least learn from Calvin that we must remember that the body of Christ is the human body that was assumed by the Son of God, in which Christ became the sinner in our place, and died for us, and in which He rose and ascended to the Father to be our Intercessor. That was Calvin's starting point for his understanding of the Christian life and of the Church, and we have to ask ourselves whether we can have any other starting point than his, whether his starting point must not also be ours because it is that of the Bible: Christ as our representative, Christ in our place.

THE AUTHOR

PAUL MATTHEWS VAN BUREN, of Glendale, Ohio, U.S.A., was born on April 20, 1924, in Norfolk, Virginia, to Harold S. van Buren of Glendale, Ohio, manufacturer with the Procter and Gamble Company, and Charlotte Matthews van Buren. He attended the Glendale Public School and the Cincinnati Country Day School, 1930-1938, and St. Paul's School in Concord, New Hampshire, from 1938-1942. He entered Harvard College in the summer of 1942, but left after one semester to serve in the United States Coast Guard, transferring in 1943 to the U.S. Naval Air Force. In 1945 he returned to Harvard to study political philosophy, graduating with honours in 1948.

From 1948 to 1951 he studied at the Episcopal Theological School, Cambridge, Massachusetts, graduating with honours. From 1951 to 1954, he studied at the University of Basel under Professor Karl Barth. Having completed the work for the doctorate, he went with his wife, Anne, whom he married in 1948, and his two daughters, Alice and Eleanor, who were born in Basel, to Detroit, Michigan, where he served as Co-rector in a 'team ministry' at St. Thomas' Episcopal Church, a small city parish. In February, 1956, he went as Curate to St. Paul's Cathedral, Detroit. His son, Philip, was born March 27, 1956, in Detroit.

BIBLIOGRAPHY

CALVIN, J. *Ioannis Calvini Opera*, in the *Corpus Reformatorum*, ed. G. Baum, E. Cunitz and E. Reuss, Brunswick, 1869-96. (Abbreviated *C.R.* in the notes.)

—— *Opera Selecta*, ed. P. Barth and W. Niesel, Munich, 1926-52.

—— *Œuvres de Jean Calvin*, ed. Société Calviniste de France, Paris, 1934-36.

—— The English versions of the *Institutes* (by J. Allen) and the *Commentaries* (Calvin Translation Society) have been helpful, but I have felt it necessary to make my own translations, for the sake of greater fidelity to the original.

ANSELM OF CANTERBURY. *Cur Deus Homo*, ed. H. Laemmer, Berlin, 1857.

PETER LOMBARD. *Libri IV sententiarum*, ed. PP. Collegii S. Bonaventurae, Ad Claras Aquas, 1916.

THOMAS AQUINAS. *Summa theologica*, ed. S. E. Fretté and P. Maré, Paris, 1871-73.

The following books on Calvin's theology I have read wholly or in part; however, I have tried to base my work solely on the writings of Calvin himself, without reference to any secondary interpretations.

NIESEL, W. *Die Christologie Calvins*, Munich, 1938.

PARKER, T. H. L. *The Doctrine of the Knowledge of God; a Study in the Theology of John Calvin*, Edinburgh, 1952.

TORRANCE, T. F. *Calvin's Doctrine of Man*, London, 1949.

WENDEL, F. *Calvin, sources et évolution de sa pensée religieuse*, Paris, 1950. (A very full bibliography of Calvin studies is given by Prof. Wendel.)

INDEX